First World War
and Army of Occupation
War Diary
France, Belgium and Germany

39 DIVISION
118 Infantry Brigade,
Brigade Machine Gun Company
and Brigade Trench Mortar Battery
27 August 1914 - 28 February 1918

WO95/2591/4-5

The Naval & Military Press Ltd
www.nmarchive.com
Published in association with The National Archives

Published by

The Naval & Military Press Ltd

Unit 10 Ridgewood Industrial Park,

Uckfield, East Sussex,

TN22 5QE England

Tel: +44 (0) 1825 749494

www.naval-military-press.com

www.nmarchive.com

This diary has been reprinted in facsimile from the original. Any imperfections are inevitably reproduced and the quality may fall short of modern type and cartographic standards.

© Crown Copyright
Images reproduced by permission of The National Archives, London, England, 2015.

Contents

Document type	Place/Title	Date From	Date To
Heading	WO95/2591/4 118 Bde MG Coy. May 1916-Feb 1918 39 Div-118 Inf Bde		
Heading	39th Division 118th Infy Bde 118th Machine Gun Coy. Mar 1916-Feb 1918		
Heading	118th Brigade. 39th Division. Formed 21st March 1916 118th Brigade Machine Gun Company 21st To 31st March 1916		
Heading	War Diary Of 118 Machine Gun Company From 21 March 1916 To 31 March 1916		
War Diary	Wallon Chappel (C.4.C.8.6. France. Sheet 36)	21/03/1916	25/03/1916
War Diary	Les Lauriers	26/03/1916	31/03/1916
Heading	118th Brigade. 39th Division. 118th Brigade Machine Gun Company April 1916		
War Diary	Lavante (M, 8.d) Sheet 36 S.W)	01/04/1916	06/04/1916
War Diary	Merville	07/04/1916	14/04/1916
War Diary	Vielle Chapelle	15/04/1916	16/04/1916
War Diary	Le Hamel (X. 20.d)	17/04/1916	19/04/1916
War Diary	Le Hamel	20/04/1916	22/04/1916
War Diary	Locon (W.L.C.)	23/04/1916	30/04/1916
Heading	118th Brigade. 39th Division. 118th Brigade Machine Gun Company May 1916		
Miscellaneous	D.A.G. 3rd Echelon	01/05/1916	01/05/1916
War Diary	Gorre (F.4.C. Ref Bethune Combined Sheet)	01/05/1916	27/05/1916
War Diary	Ferme De Roi (E.L.C)	28/05/1916	31/05/1916
Heading	118th Brigade. 39th Division. 118th Brigade Machine Gun Company June 1916		
Miscellaneous	118th Brigade. 39th Division.		
War Diary	Ferme Du. Roi E 6.C.	01/06/1916	05/06/1916
War Diary	Gorre F 4. C	06/06/1916	16/06/1916
War Diary	Near Lacouture X.3.d	17/06/1916	30/06/1916
Heading	118th Brigade. 39th Division. 118th Brigade Machine Gun Company July 1916		
Heading	War Diary Of The 118th Machine Gun Co. For the month of July 1916		
Miscellaneous	118 Inf Bde	31/07/1916	31/07/1916
Heading	War Diary of 118 Machine Gun Company for the month of July 1916 Vol. 1		
War Diary	Richbourg St. Vaast. (S.9.a.3.D)	01/07/1916	05/07/1916
War Diary	Viellechappe (X.3.d.5.5)	06/07/1916	06/07/1916
War Diary	Le Preol (F.15.d.49)	07/07/1916	14/07/1916
War Diary	Loisne (X.22.d)	15/07/1916	23/07/1916
War Diary	Gorre (F.3.d.)	24/07/1916	25/07/1916
War Diary	Bethune (E.11.d.1.9)	26/07/1916	26/07/1916
War Diary	Ecole De Jeunes Filles	27/07/1916	31/07/1916
Heading	118th Brigade. 39th Division. 118th Brigade Machine Gun Company August 1916		
Miscellaneous	118 Inf. Bde.	31/08/1916	31/08/1916
Heading	War Diary of 118 M.G. Company for month of August Vol 1		
War Diary	Loisne X. 22.d.6.7	01/08/1916	10/08/1916

War Diary	Hingette	10/08/1916	10/08/1916
War Diary	Cauchy-A-La Tour	11/08/1916	11/08/1916
War Diary	Rocourt	12/08/1916	12/08/1916
War Diary	Villers-Brulin	13/08/1916	23/08/1916
War Diary	Cannetmont	23/08/1916	23/08/1916
War Diary	Halloy (Sheet 57 D Ref. B. 17)	24/08/1916	24/08/1916
War Diary	Bus-les-Artois (J.26.)	25/08/1916	25/08/1916
War Diary	Fort Prowse	26/08/1916	26/08/1916
War Diary	France Sheet 57D S.E) Ref. Q.21.C.)	27/08/1916	31/08/1916
Heading	118th Brigade. 39th Division. 118th Brigade Machine Gun Company September 1916		
Miscellaneous	118 Inf. Bde	30/09/1916	30/09/1916
Heading	War Diary of 118 Machine Gun Company for month of September Vol. 1		
War Diary	Fort Prowse (France. Sheet 57 S.E. Q.21.C)	01/09/1916	04/09/1916
War Diary	Fort Prowse	05/09/1916	30/09/1916
Heading	118th Brigade. 39th Division. 118th Brigade Machine Gun Company October 1916		
Heading	War Diary of 118 Machine Gun Company for month of October Vol 1		
War Diary	Fort Prowse (France: Sheet St D.S.E., Q.21.C)	01/10/1916	05/10/1916
War Diary	Martinsart W.3	06/10/1916	09/10/1916
War Diary	Authville Wood (W.12 b)	10/10/1916	10/10/1916
War Diary	Authville Wood	11/10/1916	16/10/1916
War Diary	Martinsart (W.3.a.9.8)	17/10/1916	20/10/1916
War Diary	Senlis (V.10.d)	21/10/1916	28/10/1916
War Diary	Authville Q.36. C.3.3	29/10/1916	29/10/1916
War Diary	W.9.d.9.9	30/10/1916	31/10/1916
Heading	118th Brigade. 39th Division. 118th Brigade Machine Gun Company November 1916		
Heading	War Diary of 118th Machine Gun Company for the month of November 1916 Vol 7		
War Diary	Authville (Q.36.C.3.3)	01/11/1916	02/11/1916
War Diary	Senlis (V.10.d)	03/11/1916	07/11/1916
War Diary	Authville (Q.36.C.3.3)	08/11/1916	09/11/1916
War Diary	Senlis V.1.d	10/11/1916	10/11/1916
War Diary	Pioneer Rd	11/11/1916	11/11/1916
War Diary	Authville Q 36. C.3.3	12/11/1916	12/11/1916
War Diary	Paisley Dump. (Thiepval)	13/11/1916	13/11/1916
War Diary	St Pierre Divion	14/11/1916	15/11/1916
War Diary	Senlis	15/11/1916	15/11/1916
War Diary	Warloy	15/11/1916	15/11/1916
War Diary	Ref. France Sheet 57 D. 1/40000	16/11/1916	16/11/1916
War Diary	Amplier Orville Area	17/11/1916	17/11/1916
War Diary	Doullens & Candas (Lens II. Sheet)	18/11/1916	19/11/1916
War Diary	Wormhoudt	19/11/1916	26/11/1916
War Diary	Wormhoudt. Camp. F Ref 1/200000 Map. Sheet 28 (A16 C 67.)	29/11/1916	30/11/1916
Heading	118th Brigade. 39th Division. 118th Brigade Machine Gun Company December 1916		
War Diary	Decouck Farm B13 b 2.8 Ref (Belgium) Sheet 28 N.W.	01/12/1916	09/12/1916
War Diary	Decouck Farm	10/12/1916	11/12/1916
War Diary	S. Camp	12/12/1916	22/12/1916
War Diary	C. 25 Canal. Bk.	23/12/1916	31/12/1916
War Diary	Canal Bk. C 25 d. 8.4 Sheet 28 NW Edit. 3.E	01/01/1917	24/01/1917
War Diary	Brandhoek	25/01/1917	16/02/1917

War Diary	S. Camp.	17/02/1917	17/02/1917
War Diary	Y. Camp.	18/02/1917	26/02/1917
War Diary	Erie Camp G 11.C 84	27/02/1917	28/02/1917
Heading	War Diary of 118th Machine Gun Company. From:- 1st March, 1917 To 31st March 1917. (Volume-I)		
War Diary	Erie Camp (G 11 C 6.2)	01/03/1917	03/03/1917
War Diary	Zillebeke Bund	04/03/1917	07/03/1917
War Diary	Observatory Ridge Section	08/03/1917	08/03/1917
War Diary	Ypres (Hodge. Section)	09/03/1917	15/03/1917
War Diary	Erie Camp (G 11 C 62)	16/03/1917	20/03/1917
War Diary	Zillebeke Bund	21/03/1917	21/03/1917
War Diary	Zillebeke Bund. Observatory Ridge Section	22/03/1917	27/03/1917
War Diary	Ypres (Hodge Section)	28/03/1917	31/03/1917
Heading	War Diary of 118th Machine Gun Company from 1st April 1917-to. 30th April. 1917 Volume II		
War Diary	Ypres	01/04/1917	02/04/1917
War Diary	Erie Camp G 11 c 85 Sheet 28 NW	03/04/1917	03/04/1917
War Diary	Erie Camp Sheet 28 NW G 11.c.8.4	03/04/1917	04/04/1917
War Diary	Houtkerque Sheet 27 B&F	05/04/1917	07/04/1917
War Diary	Sheet 27 Btf Houtrerque	08/04/1917	14/04/1917
War Diary	Houtkerque	14/04/1917	16/04/1917
War Diary	'S' Camp (A22d83) Ref. Trench Map 28 NW 4	17/04/1917	20/04/1917
War Diary	Trench Map 28 NW 4 A22d 83 S. Camp	20/04/1917	24/04/1917
War Diary	S. Camp	24/04/1917	26/04/1917
War Diary	Coy H Q Canal Bk Sheet 28 NW A 28 C 54	27/04/1917	27/04/1917
War Diary	Canal Bk A 28 C 54 Trench Map 28 NW 4	27/04/1917	30/04/1917
War Diary	Canal Bk.	30/04/1917	30/04/1917
Heading	War Diary of 118th Machine Gun Company from 1st May 1917-to-31st May, 1917 Volume II		
War Diary	Coy H.Q. Canal Bk Hill Top Sector	01/05/1917	05/05/1917
War Diary	Coy HQ Canal Bk	05/05/1917	10/05/1917
War Diary	Canal Bk.	10/05/1917	16/05/1917
War Diary	'S' Camp. A 22d 6.3	17/05/1917	31/05/1917
Miscellaneous	Appendix A Ref Map. St. Julien	30/05/1917	30/05/1917
War Diary	War Diary of 118th Machine Gun Company from 1st June 1917 to 30th June, 1917 Volume II		
War Diary	S, Camp A 22d 8.3	01/06/1917	07/06/1917
War Diary	Wormhoudt Ref Map	08/06/1917	08/06/1917
War Diary	Hazebrouck 5a	09/06/1917	09/06/1917
War Diary	Wormhoudt	10/06/1917	10/06/1917
War Diary	Ochtezeele	11/06/1917	11/06/1917
War Diary	Esquerdes	12/06/1917	12/06/1917
War Diary	Watterdal	13/06/1917	20/06/1917
War Diary	Salperwick	21/06/1917	27/06/1917
War Diary	Salperwick C Camp a 3d 05.56	28/06/1917	28/06/1917
War Diary	Canal Bank	29/06/1917	30/06/1917
Heading	War Diary of 118th Machine Gun Company from 1st July 1917-to 31st July, 1917 Volume II		
War Diary	Coy H.Q. Canal Bank Hill Top Sector	01/07/1917	15/07/1917
War Diary	Camp A 30 Central	15/07/1917	16/07/1917
War Diary	L 17d 5.6	17/07/1917	17/07/1917
War Diary	Coy H.Q.meulle 3c 3.2-5.3	17/07/1917	17/07/1917
War Diary	Coy H.Q Moulle 3c 3.2-5.3	18/07/1917	22/07/1917
War Diary	9 Coy HQ Z Camp 24 90 Bde	23/07/1917	23/07/1917
War Diary	Z Camp	24/07/1917	28/07/1917
War Diary	Z Camp S Camp	29/07/1917	29/07/1917

War Diary	S Camp & Canal Bank Duj-eur a 2	30/07/1917	31/07/1917
Operation(al) Order(s)	118th Machine Gun Company Order No. 31	02/07/1917	02/07/1917
Miscellaneous	Machine Gun Table		
Heading	War Diary of 118th Machine Gun Company from 1st August 1917-to 31st August 1917 Volume II		
War Diary	Canteen March C 17 b 65 15	01/08/1917	02/08/1917
War Diary	Dugout 116 Canal Bank W	03/08/1917	06/08/1917
War Diary	R20 c 5.4	10/08/1917	13/08/1917
War Diary	Ridge Wood N 5 c 0.5	14/08/1917	18/08/1917
War Diary	Ridge Wood N 5 c 0.5 Coy HQ At Bluff Trenches	18/08/1917	19/08/1917
War Diary	Bluff Tunnels Coy HQ	19/08/1917	20/08/1917
War Diary	Coy HQ Bluff Tunnels	21/08/1917	26/08/1917
War Diary	Ridge Wood N 5 C O. 5	27/08/1914	31/08/1914
Heading	War Diary of 118th Machine Gun Company From 1st September-to 30th September 1917 Volume II		
War Diary	Ridge Wood N 5 C 0 5	01/09/1917	03/09/1917
War Diary	Larch Wood I 29c. 1585	04/09/1917	07/09/1917
War Diary	Ridge Wood N 5 c 0 5	08/09/1917	16/09/1917
War Diary	M 86 8.3	17/09/1917	18/09/1917
War Diary	M. 9 b Central	19/09/1917	20/09/1917
War Diary	M 9 b-Central J 25 c 5 1	21/09/1917	21/09/1917
War Diary	G 25 B 5.1	22/09/1917	23/09/1917
War Diary	G 25 B 5.1 a G 3 0 C 9.9	24/09/1917	24/09/1917
War Diary	G 30 C 9.9	25/09/1917	28/09/1917
War Diary	M 13 b 9.9	28/09/1917	30/09/1917
Heading	War Diary of 118th Machine Gun Company from 1st October to 31st October 1917 Volume II		
War Diary	M 13 b 9.9 fronter Camp	01/10/1917	13/10/1917
War Diary	M 13 b 9.9	14/10/1917	15/10/1917
War Diary	N 15 a 8.4	16/10/1917	19/10/1917
War Diary	Shunabeng fust	20/10/1917	20/10/1917
War Diary	M 15 a 84	21/10/1917	23/10/1917
War Diary	Chippewa Camp M 6 a 5.7	28/10/1917	29/10/1917
War Diary	Chippewa Camp M 6 a 5.7. & Dug-Out at Hedge Sheet Tunnels	29/10/1917	29/10/1917
War Diary	Hedge Sheet	30/10/1917	31/10/1917
Heading	War Diary of 118th Machine Gun Company from 1st November 1917 to 30th November 1917 Volume II		
War Diary	Hedge Street	01/11/1917	04/11/1917
War Diary	Chippewa Camp M. 6.a. 5.6	05/11/1917	08/11/1917
War Diary	N. 5.d.9.9	09/11/1917	10/11/1917
War Diary	J. 19 b 35.90	11/11/1917	15/11/1917
War Diary	Chippewa Camp M 6 a 5 6	16/11/1917	19/11/1917
War Diary	J 19 b 49	20/11/1917	26/11/1917
War Diary	J 19 b 49 & Cheppeua Camp	26/11/1917	27/11/1917
War Diary	Q 15b 0.6	27/11/1917	30/11/1917
Heading	War Diary of 118th Machine Gun Company From 1st December 1917 to 31st December 1917 Volume II		
War Diary	Eecke Area Q 15 Central	01/12/1917	08/12/1917
War Diary	Watterdal	09/12/1917	09/12/1917
War Diary	Brunembert	10/12/1917	29/12/1917
War Diary	Watterdal	30/12/1917	31/12/1917
War Diary	War Diary of 118th Machine Gun Company From 1st January 1918 to 31st January 1918 Volume II		
War Diary	Lart	01/01/1918	01/01/1918
War Diary	Canal Bank	02/01/1918	08/01/1918

War Diary	Alberta	09/01/1918	09/01/1918
War Diary	Alberta C.11.c. B.6	09/01/1918	15/01/1918
War Diary	Alberta	15/01/1918	16/01/1918
War Diary	Siege Camp	17/01/1918	17/01/1918
War Diary	B.20.d.8.7	18/01/1918	21/01/1918
War Diary	Houtkerque E 13 d 1.0	22/01/1918	25/01/1918
War Diary	Bray	26/01/1918	29/01/1918
War Diary	Sorelle Grand	30/01/1918	31/01/1918
Heading	War Diary of 118th Machine Gun Company from 1st February 1918 to 28th February 1918 Volume II		
War Diary	Soul. Le. Grand V.R d 95.30 Q29 a 8.0	01/02/1918	03/02/1918
War Diary	Q29 a 8.0	03/02/1918	28/02/1918
Heading	WO95/2591/5 118 Bde T.M. Batty Jul-Aug 1916 39 Div-118 Inf Bde		
Heading	39th Division 118th Infy Bde Trench Mortar Bty Jly-Aug 1916		
Miscellaneous	116th Infantry Brigade	30/06/1916	30/06/1916
Miscellaneous	Headquarters, 39th Division	19/08/1916	19/08/1916
Miscellaneous	D.A.G. 3rd Echelon Base.	19/08/1916	19/08/1916
War Diary	Vis The Chapelly	01/07/1916	31/07/1916
War Diary	Festubert.	01/08/1916	15/08/1916
War Diary	Bethonsart	16/08/1916	23/08/1916
War Diary	Canettemont	24/08/1916	24/08/1916
War Diary	Halloy	25/08/1916	25/08/1916
War Diary	Bus-Les-Artois	26/08/1916	26/08/1916
War Diary	Mailly-Maillet	26/08/1916	31/08/1916

WO95/2591 – 4

118 Bde MG Coy.

Mar 1916 – Feb 1918

39 Div – 118 Inf Bde

39TH DIVISION
118TH INFY BDE

118TH MACHINE GUN COY.

MAR 1916 - FEB 1918.

118th Brigade.
39th Division.

Formed 21st March 1916.

118th BRIGADE MACHINE GUN COMPANY

21st to 31st MARCH 1916 ::

CONFIDENTIAL.

WAR DIARY

OF

118 MACHINE GUN COMPANY.

FROM. 21 March 1916
TO. ~~8th April~~ 1916.
31 March 1916

118TH
No.
DATE 3-5-16
MACHINE GUN COY.

W Andrew Capt.
OC 118 M.G. Coy

Army Form C. 2118.

Machigils

WAR DIARY
or
INTELLIGENCE SUMMARY

(Erase heading not required.)

Instructions regarding War Diaries and Intelligence Summaries are contained in F. S. Regs., Part II. and the Staff Manual respectively. Title Pages will be prepared in manuscript.

Place	Date	Hour	Summary of Events and Information	Remarks and references to Appendices.
WAILLON CHAPPEL (C.4.C.8.6. FRANCE Sheet 36A)	March 1916 21		118th Machine Gun Company formed out of the Machine Gun Sections of the battalions in the 118 Inf Bde. The men are these months experienced of Machine Gun work in the trenches. supported by a nucleus of	
	22 23		Coy being organised + guns + stores beginning to arrive.	
	24			
	25		Coy moved to billets in FARM. K.21.a.9.6 (Ref FRANCE sheet 36A) at LES LAURIERS near MERVILLE at 11.30 am.	
LES LAURIERS.	26 27 28 29 30 31		Coy was organising + training	

W Andrew Capt
OC 118 M.G. Coy

118th Brigade.
39th Division.

118th BRIGADE MACHINE GUN COMPANY

APRIL 1916

April 1916

WAR DIARY or INTELLIGENCE SUMMARY

Army Form C. 2118.

Place	Date	Hour	Summary of Events and Information	Remarks and references to Appendices
LES LABOURES LAVANTIE (M.S.a) Sheet 36 S.W.	1.4.16		Coy moved up into the line & relieved the 57 M.G. Coy. New headquarters at M.S.a. 4.9. (Ref. Map FRUNGE sheet 36 S.W.) The 118 Inf Bde took over the MOATED GRANGE sector in front of LAVANTIE. The line of resistance was a line of Breast work, the second a number of strong points in the front line I had four guns. These guns remained in their double emplacements which were closed & mostly of concrete, by day & fired from open emplacements by night. They fired an average of about 500 rounds per gun per night across the front of craters at a gap in the GERMAN Wire. Each gun had a specified task. There was no evidence that the enemy have located any of our guns while we silenced one of their machine guns firing with only any nightfiring seen.	
	2.4.16 3.4.16 4.4.16 5.4.16 6.4.16		Nothing of importance to record.	
			Were relieved by 57 M.G. Coy, part of the relief taking place by day & part by night. Arrived at new billet at FARMES PURESBECQUES on MERVILLE for rest at 11 p.m.	
MERVILLE	7.4.16 8.4.16 9.4.16		Organization & training carried on.	
	10.4.16		Lieut. H. Andrew (Commanding) reported sick and moved to 32nd C.C. Station at Vernel. 2nd Lieut. W. GORE assumed temporary command.	

April 1916

Army Form C. 2118.

WAR DIARY
or
INTELLIGENCE SUMMARY.

(Erase heading not required.)

Place	Date	Hour	Summary of Events and Information	Remarks and references to Appendices
MERVILLE	11-4-16			
	12-4-16		Company training continued	
	13-4-16			
	14-4-16	11.a.m	Moved to new billets via LESTREM to VIELLE CHAPELLE X.4.c.6.3. arriving at 3 pm	
VIELLE CHAPELLE	15-4-16	7-30 am	No 1 Section with 4 guns to complete in charge of 2nd Lieut N.E. BEAUMONT moved to LOCON X.7.c.9.1. with orders to report to G.O.C. 116th Brigade for duty	
		2 pm	3 guns + teams of No 3 Section moved to FESTUBERT, and took over emplacements in le PLANTIN NORTH A.2.c.2.5, FESTUBERT, S.25.d. + FESTUBERT EAST S.26.c.4.4. relieving LEWIS GUNS of 15th Welsh Regt. Relief completed at 4 pm	
	16-4-16	11 am	Moved to new billets via ZELOBES LOCON to le HAMEL X.20.d.5.5. arriving at 1 pm	
le HAMEL (X.20.d.)	17-4-16	6 pm	No 2 Section with 4 guns + teams complete in charge of Lieut R.T. ASHETON and 2nd Lieut J.C. PRAIN, moved to FESTUBERT SECTION, and took over emplacements to Nos R.1. R.4. R.5. + R.11 in O-B LINE then vacant.	
			All guns of No 2 + 3 SECTION occupied concrete BATTLE EMPLACEMENTS, and there has been no occasion to fire.	
	18-4-16		Lieut W.C. ANDREW reported for duty at 5 pm 18/4/16 and resumes command as from 32. C.C.S today	

Army Form C. 2118.

WAR DIARY
or
INTELLIGENCE SUMMARY

April 1916

(Erase heading not required.)

Place	Date	Hour	Summary of Events and Information	Remarks and references to Appendices
LE HAMEL	20.4.16 21.4.16 22.4.16		Time spent in improving the wire & in perfecting the scheme of defence. The main work starting was an emplacement in FIFE ROAD at Point A.2.06.25 firing S.E. across a gap in the OLD BRITISH LINE. We were the first Machine Gun Company to occupy this sector	
LOCON (W.C.C)	23.4.16		Was relieved by the 117 M.G. Coy relief being completed at 4 p.m. We then moved over to reserve billets at LOCON in AREA W.C.C.	
	24.4.16 25.4.16 26.4.16 27.4.16 28.4.16 29.4.16 30.4.16		As the 117 M.G. Coy is almost untrained this company supplies half gun teams for each gun & 1 N.C.O. for every two guns. We also supply guns etc & transport. So now we have the guns & transport of two sections with 1 section of gunners in FESTUBERT SECTOR, & 1 complete section in GUINCHY SECTOR. Guns & men not attached to 117 Inf Bde or 116 Inf Bde in Reserve.	

W Andrew Capt.
OC 118 M.G. Coy

118th Brigade.
39th Division.

118th BRIGADE MACHINE GUN COMPANY

MAY 1916

D.A.G.
  3rd Echelon.

Herewith War Diary for month of May.

1.5.16

W Andrew Capt.
O.C. 118 M.G. Coy.

118 Bde M G Coy
Vol 1

WAR DIARY or INTELLIGENCE SUMMARY

Army Form C. 2118.

(Erase heading not required.)

Place	Date	Hour	Summary of Events and Information	Remarks and references to Appendices
GORRE [F.4.c Réf] BETHUNE COMBINED SHEET	1.5.16		Moved from LOCON into GIVENCHY SECTOR, arriving at new Headquarters in FARM at F.4.c. at 1 p.m. The Company took over the machine gun work which since 15.4.16 has been undertaken by No 1 Section under 2/Lt BEAUMONT. The 117 M.G. Coy consisted of Lt. for the most part, untrained or partially trained men, as the company took over the divisional front, seven guns being in the FESTUBERT SECTOR, & four in the GIVENCHY SECTOR. We remained Divisional troops with headquarters at GORRE till the 25th inst. Lts Oppheim & men of the 117 M.G. Coy were attached to this company for duty & instruction.	
	2.5.16 3.5.16 4.5.16 5.5.16 6.5.16		Indirect fire carried out in GIVENCHY SECTOR at night. Four guns complete under Lieut. ASSHETON proceeded to LOCON to form a Divisional Machine Gun School. Two instructors of whom two were N.C.O.'s went with guns.	
	7.5.16 to 27.5.16		Indirect fire continued at GIVENCHY, & also started from the Old British Line at FESTUBERT. We enfiladed the GERMAN Front Line on GIVENCHY RIDGE at night from the O.B.L. & prepared positions & made out cards for enfilading the remainder of the GERMAN Front Line & communication trenches on the Divisional front. I was officiating Divisional Machine Gun Officer (temp.) & during the month, worked on a Divisional scheme of M.G. defence.	

WAR DIARY
or
INTELLIGENCE SUMMARY

Army Form C. 2118.

Place	Date	Hour	Summary of Events and Information	Remarks and references to Appendices
	27.5.16 (Contd.)		The 117 M.G. Coy which had arrived from GRANTHAM on the 19th inst & had been in line for instruction, took over the GIVENCHY SECTOR, the relief being completed at 4 p.m.	
FERME DE ROI (H.Q.)	28.5.16		The 118 Inf. Bde which was in FESTUBERT SECTOR, received orders to have one to the 106 Inf. Bde - to hold itself in instant readiness for action. The 101 M.G. Coy relieved this company the same evening, the relief being completed at 2.30 a.m. & the company moved to reserve billets at FERME DE ROI, near BETHUNE, at E.6.C., the move being completed at 4 a.m. 29th inst. I received orders to reconnoitre the roads & country up to & in the bivouac area immediately south of the BETHUNE - LA BASSÉS ROAD, which I did. 2 Lt William Jas has been promoted temporary Lieutenant to be second in command of the company. As the Brigade is now on special duty, I cease to be Div. M.G. Officer.	
	29.5.16 30.5.16 31.5.16		Reorganised the company which had not been together for some weeks. The Company was inspected by Brigadier General T. P. Bennington, B.D.C. 118 Inf. Bde. The company is bivouacced & held in readiness for immediate action.	

W. Ambrose Capt

118th Brigade,
39th Division.

118th BRIGADE MACHINE GUN COMPANY

JUNE 1916

118th Brigade.
39th Division.

Army Form C. 2118.

WAR DIARY
or
INTELLIGENCE SUMMARY
(Erase heading not required.)

Instructions regarding War Diaries and Intelligence Summaries are contained in F.S. Regs., Part II. and the Staff Manual respectively. Title Pages will be prepared in manuscript.

Place	Date	Hour	Summary of Events and Information	Remarks and references to Appendices
FERME DU ROI E.6.C.	1/6/16	10. a.m.	Company was inspected by Brigadier General T.P. Barrington G.O.C. 118th Infantry Brigade	
do	1/6/16 to 5/6/16		The Company bivouaced in Field in readiness for immediate action. Capt. W. Bristow proceeds on leave to U. Kingdom. Lieut. W. GORE assumes temporary command Coy	
GORRE F 4. C	6-6-16	7. a.m.	The Company moved from FERME DU ROI, E.6.C. to GORRE, and relieved the 117th Coy M.G. Corps in GIVENCHY SECTION. 3 Sections with 12 guns taking over positions in the line, and one section with 4 guns remaining at Hd Qrs GORRE in reserve. The relief was duly carried out and completed by 3 p.m.	
	6/6/16 to 16/6/16		During this period Company in GIVENCHY-FRONT, with guns as above, 2 guns fired nightly, Relieved fire on Communication Trenches, Roads to behind Enemy Lines.	
	16.6.16		Company relieved by 19th Coy M.G. Corps, all sections proceeding taken over but 1 section with 4 guns of this Company remained for special duty in connection with Special arm Enemy trenches on night of 16/17th June and fired 10,750 rounds by indirect fire on Enemy Communication Trenches Roads, so along the whole front. Articles, T. Mortars, & M.Guns opened fire at 1 am night of 16/17th June, a mine was exploded by us at 1.9 a.m. The Raiding party moves forward at 1.8 am. Successfully entered Enemy trenches, killed & wounded 25 to 30, and brought back one wounded prisoner. Fire of M. Guns was kept up continuously from 1 am to 1-50 am. The section dismantled guns at 2 am and moved out of the line to join rest of Company at GORRE	

2449 Wt. W14957/M90 750,000 1/16 J.B.C. & A. Forms/C.2118/12.

WAR DIARY
or
INTELLIGENCE SUMMARY

Army Form C. 2118.

Place	Date	Hour	Summary of Events and Information	Remarks and references to Appendices
Near LACOUTURE X.3.d.	17.6.16	4-30 am	Company moved from GORRE, F.4.c. to X.3.d., and became attached to 116th Infy Brigade, for duty, and relieved portion of 104th and 105th Coys M.G. Corps in the FERME DU BOIS. Section. 3 Lectures with 16 Guns took over positions in the line, and 1 Section with 4 Guns in reserve at X.3.d.	
do	19-6-16	9 am	Company relieved in the FERME DU BOIS, Sections by the 118th Coy M.G. Corps, the Sections on the line on completion of relief at 1-30 pm returned to Company HQrs at X.3.d. — under orders of G.O.C. 118th Infy Brigade. Capt H Andrews having reported back from leave, resumed Command.	
do	19.6.16			
	20.6.16 to 23.6.16		Coy reorganising & training with a view to open warfare, while acting as Divl Reserve.	
	24.6.16		Bde Horse Show held. A Coy mule got first prize.	
	25.6.16 to 28.6.16		Coy under orders to move at 4.8 hrs notice. Training with a view to open warfare continued.	
	29.6.16		Received orders to be prepared to move at 1 hrs notice from 8 p.m. They were due to attempt made on the night of the 29/30 to capture & hold about 500 yds of the German line in the FERME DU BOIS section the attempt was made by the 116 Inf. Bde.	

Army Form C.2118.

WAR DIARY
or
INTELLIGENCE SUMMARY
(Erase heading not required.)

Instructions regarding War Diaries and Intelligence Summaries are contained in F. S. Regs., Part II. and the Staff Manual respectively. Title Pages will be prepared in manuscript.

Place	Date	Hour	Summary of Events and Information	Remarks and references to Appendices
NEAR LACOUTURE X.3.d.	June 30.6.16		Attempt to hold German front line failed. We are still attempting to recover some at / his notice. Training continues.	

W Andrew Capt.
O.C. 118 M.G. Coy

118th Brigade.
39th Division.

118th BRIGADE MACHINE GUN COMPANY

JULY 1916

Confidential

War Diary
- of the -
118th Machine Gun Co.
for the month of
July 1916

39/118 M.G.C. July Vol 5

118 Inf Bde

31·7·16

Herewith War Diary for the
Month of July.

W Andrew Capt
118th M. G. Coy.

War Diary.

of

118 Machine Gun Company.

for

The Month of July, 1916.

VOL. 1.

Army Form C. 2118.

WAR DIARY
or
INTELLIGENCE SUMMARY
(Erase heading not required.)

10

Place	Date	Hour	Summary of Events and Information	Remarks and references to Appendices
RICHBOURG ST VAAST. (S.2.a.3,D)	July 1916 1		This company relieved the 116 M.G. Coy & took over M.G. positions in the FERME DU BOIS. SECTOR, the relief being completed at 9.15 p.m. 5 guns were in emplacements in the front line, 7, in keeps in support & 4 guns in reserve at RICHBOURG ST VAAST.	
	2		Indirect fire organised, fire guns in night firing positions in rear sec. etc. communication trenches, roads & light railways & possible dumps.	
	3.		Indirect fire continued. Loophole of emplacement in front line blown in. No casualties.	
	4 } 5 }		Indirect fire continued. Guns on front line also fired at night searching the enemys wire & parapet.	
VIELLECHAPPELLE (X.3.d.55)	6		Relieved during the night by the 184th M.G. Coy, the company moving back to Billets near VIELLE CHAPPELLE (X.3.a.3,3.)	
LE PREOL (F.15.A.4.9)	7		Coy moved out 6.30p.m. to relieve the 19th M.G. Coy in GIVENCHY, Relief was completed at 1 a.m. on the 8th. 10 guns were put into GIVENCHY & 4 into CUINCHY, 2 remaining in reserve at LE PREOL. 14 guns in the front line.	
	8 to 14th		Indirect fire carried out every night. GERMAN prisoners reports that certain roads & communication trenches were used mostly when reliefs were being carried out. Particular attention was paid to these places when firing at night	

2449 Wt. W14957/M90 750,000 1/16 J.B.C. & A. Forms/C.2118/12.

Army Form C. 2118.

WAR DIARY
or
INTELLIGENCE SUMMARY

(Erase heading not required.)

Instructions regarding War Diaries and Intelligence Summaries are contained in F. S. Regs., Part II. and the Staff Manual respectively. Title Pages will be prepared in manuscript.

Place	Date	Hour	Summary of Events and Information	Remarks and references to Appendices
LE PREOL (F.15.d.4.9)	July 12.		All available Officers, N.C.O's & men went into a Gas Chamber with Box respirators.	
	13 14		Fine weather continues.	
LOISNE (X.22.d)	15.	11 p.m.	The 4 guns in CUINCHY were relieved by the 23rd M.G. Coy.	
			On completion of relief, these guns were moved directly into FESTUBERT, relieving the 114 M.G. Coy. These guns took over emplacements in the (O.B.L.) the support line. Relief was completed at 2 a.m on the 16th inst.	
			Headquarters were moved to LOISNE (X.22.a)	
	16 17 18 19 20 21 22 23		Weather fine, carried out email night by 2 guns in GIVENCHY & 2 in FESTUBERT	
GORRE (F.3.a.)	24	11 p.m	Guns in FESTUBERT were relieved by the 116 M.G. Coy, the relief being completed at 11 p.m.	
			Headquarters were moved to GORRE (F.3.a)	

Army Form C. 2118.

WAR DIARY
or
INTELLIGENCE SUMMARY
(Erase heading not required.)

12.

Place	Date	Hour	Summary of Events and Information	Remarks and references to Appendices
GORRE (F.3.d.)	1916 July 25		night firing continued	
BETHUNE 26 (E.11.d.1.9.) ECOLE DE JEUNES FILLES	26		Company relieved by 119 M.G. Coy, the relief being complete at 2 p.m. On being relieved, the company moved into Billets in BETHUNE.	
	27 28 29 30		Time spent in reorganising company, + in full days (open warfare practice) on ridge overand BETHUNE.	
	31.		Brig. notice - General E.H. Ynich-Hatten C.M.G, D.S.O, inspected the company during field operations.	

W Andrew Capt.
O.C. 118 M.G. Coy.

118th Brigade.
39th Division.

118th BRIGADE MACHINE GUN COMPANY

AUGUST 1 9 1 6

118 Inf. Bde.

Herewith War Diary for month
of August.

31.8.16   W Andrew Capt.
                   OC 118 M.G. Coy

<u>Confidential</u>

War Diary
of
<u>118 M.G. Company.</u>

for month of

<u>August</u>

<u>Vol. 1.</u>

Vol 4

WAR DIARY or INTELLIGENCE SUMMARY

Army Form C. 2118.

13

Place	Date	Hour	Summary of Events and Information	Remarks and references to Appendices
	August 1916			
LOISNE	1		Relieved the 116 M.G. Coy in FESTUBERT the relief being completed at 8 p.m.	
X.22.d.6.7	2		7 guns are in the O.B.L (support line), 6 in the Village line, 3 guns being in reserve. No guns were put in the front line as this consists of a series of islands.	
	3		Indirect fire carried out. Range Cards + Charts supplied for all emplacements in the 1 Brigade Area, also double Blanket over doors & arc of anti gun solution.	
	4			
	5		Indirect fire carried out.	
	6			
	7		Indirect fire carried out. A gun was taken down to Interval N° 11 each night. This gun working in conjunction with a patrol supplied with a telephone fired at a gap in the German wire when a working party was noticed there.	
	8			
	9			
	10		Company relieved in FESTUBERT by 93 M.G. Coy, the relief being complete at 3 p.m. On completion of relief, company moved to billets at HINGETTE, near BETHUNE, arriving there at 9 p.m.	
HINGETTE				
CAUCHY-A-	11		Brigade moved to billets about AUCHY, the company proceeding at 2.15 p.m. & arriving in new billets at 8.15 p.m.	
TOUR				

Army Form C. 2118.

WAR DIARY
or
INTELLIGENCE SUMMARY.
(Erase heading not required.)

14.

Place	Date	Hour	Summary of Events and Information	Remarks and references to Appendices
	August			
ROCOURT.	12		Company paraded at 2 p.m. & marched with Brigade to new billets, arriving there at 7.30 p.m. ROCOURT is 7 miles E.N.E. of ST. POL.	
VILLERS-BRULIN	13		Coy move off at 6.10 am to billets at VILLERS-BRULIN & commenced training in the Attack & Open Warfare. Arrived in new billets at 9am. VILLERS-BRULIN is mid-way between ARRAS & ST. POL, + 3 miles N. of ARRAS - ST POL road.	
	14 to 22		Training continued at Div. Training Ground. Company trained independently for the first 6 days, & for the remaining two, section work in co-operation with other battalions in Attack Scheme.	
	23		Company paraded at 8.30 am. & moved with brigade to new billets at CANNETMONT (five miles E. of FRÉVENT), arriving in new billets at 2 p.m.	
CANNETMONT				
HALLOY (SHEET 57D) (Ref. B. 17.)	24		Company paraded at 8.45 am & marched with the Brigade to new billets at HALLOY, arriving at 2 p.m.	

Army Form C. 2118.

WAR DIARY
or
INTELLIGENCE SUMMARY.
(Erase heading not required.)

Instructions regarding War Diaries and Intelligence Summaries are contained in F.S. Regs., Part II. and the Staff Manual respectively. Title pages will be prepared in manuscript.

Place	Date	Hour	Summary of Events and Information	Remarks and references to Appendices
	August			
BUS-LES-ARTOIS (J. 26.)	25	8.45 am	Company paraded at 8.45 am & marched to new billets at BUS-LES-ARTOIS, arriving at 2 p.m.	
FORT PROWSE FRANCE SHEET 57 D S.E Rd	26	6 am	Company paraded at 6 am. & proceeded to relieve the 16th M.G. Coy, immediately N. of the River ANCRE, relief being completed at 1 p.m.	
Q. 21. C.)	27 to 31		Arrangements made for GERMAN front Diversion of Trenches. Two sections are detailed to cover left flank of the Division by sweeping communication & ground on left of attack. Two sections are held in divisional reserve supporting the 116 & 117 Inf. Bdes in the assault of the	

W Andrew Capt.
O.C. 118 M.G. Coy.

118th Brigade.
39th Division.

118th BRIGADE MACHINE GUN COMPANY

SEPTEMBER 1916

118 R&F   Vol 5

118th
No. ....
DATE 30.9.16
MACHINE GUN COY

118 Inf. Bde.

Herewith War Diary for the month of ~~August~~ Septr.

McAndrew Capt. Cmdg.
118th M. G. Coy.

WAR DIARY

of

118 MACHINE GUN COMPANY

for month of

SEPTEMBER ~~AUGUST~~

VOL I.

WAR DIARY or INTELLIGENCE SUMMARY

Army Form C. 2118.

Place	Date	Hour	Summary of Events and Information	Remarks and references to Appendices
FORT PROWSE FRANCE, SHEET 57^D S.E. Q.21.C.)	Sept. 1 2		Arrangement for supporting the attack of the 116th & 117th Inf. Bdes. continued, 8 guns covering the left flank of the attacking brigades. Night firing carried out regularly on enemy communications & roads in the valley of the ANCRE.	
	3.		116 + 117 Inf Bdes attacked the front line again & of trenches from the River ANCRE on the right to trench running from Q.17.b.14 to Q.17.d.5.8 (Ref. Map. FRANCE, sheet 57^D S.E.) Attack commenced at 5.10 a.m. 8 guns of this company opened fire at 5.10 a.m. on the communication trenches & ground to the left of the Div^l objective & continuous firing till 2 p.m. Rounds fired were 80,000. Objective was not held, & infantry retired on old positions. In the evening the 116th & 117th Inf. Bdes were withdrawn & the 118th Inf. Bde continued a rifle the line. Night firing carried on as usual.	
	4.		During the day men could be seen moving up the GERMAN trenches— owing to the trenches being heavily destroyed. A gun was set on a large gap & for several days enemies or parties passing thereabouts could live were inflicted, 5 being observed in one day.	

Army Form C. 2118.

WAR DIARY
or
INTELLIGENCE SUMMARY.
(Erase heading not required.)

Instructions regarding War Diaries and Intelligence Summaries are contained in F. S. Regs., Part II. and the Staff Manual respectively. Title pages will be prepared in manuscript.

Place	Date	Hour	Summary of Events and Information	Remarks and references to Appendices
FORT PROWSE	Sept. 5		Night firing continued.	17
	6 to 13		Trenches which had been dug in NO MANS LAND as "jumping off" trenches were taken on the firing & support lines after the assault. The scheme of M.G. Defense & Lewis Guns continued to submit a new scheme of M.G. defence. Sniping by day & ordinary night firing carried on.	
	14.		To protect planting 1/4 Cheshire Regt. on a raid carried out by daylight, a gun was brought forward to the firing line on each flank of the raiding party. These guns traversed outwards whilst the infantry were advancing, & whilst they were retiring traversed inwards to protect their rear. Sniping by day & ordinary night firing carried on.	
	15 to 18			
	19.		118 Inf. Bde. evacuated the front, taking over the "Y" RAVINE SECTION, the Bde. Section on the immediate left of this brigade.	

Army Form C. 2118.

WAR DIARY
~~INTELLIGENCE SUMMARY~~.
(Erase heading not required.)

Instructions regarding War Diaries and Intelligence Summaries are contained in F. S. Regs., Part II. and the Staff Manual respectively. Title pages will be prepared in manuscript.

Place	Date	Hour	Summary of Events and Information	Remarks and references to Appendices
FORT PROWSE (Centre)	Sept. 19		Two sections of the 117 M.G. Coy were attached to this company (the 117 M.G. Coy having been relieved by this company) & remained in position in the line. The four guns of the company were also put into the line, thus having every available gun forward. Company by day & ordinary night firing continued.	
	20 } 21 }			
	22.		Scheme of offence submitted to the Brigade for the HAMEL & Y RAVINE sectors (the sections held by the brigade). Preparations to support attack by II Corps on THIEPVAL & also attack to envelope THIEPVAL from the south.	
	23 } 24 } 25 }			
	26.		II Corps attacked at 12.35 p.m. 9 guns of this company open fire on that area & searched the roads in the valley of the ANGRE & the communication trenches in the southern slope of the valley. 5 guns also also the communication trenches & roads in rear of enemy line on our own front. Fire was kept up till	

T2134. Wt. W708—776. 500000. 4/15. Sir J. C. & S.

Army Form C. 2118.

WAR DIARY
or
INTELLIGENCE SUMMARY.
(Erase heading not required.)

Place	Date	Hour	Summary of Events and Information	Remarks and references to Appendices
FORT PROWSE	Sept. 26 (contd.)	7/pm	100,000 rounds were fired. During the night, fire was continued by 3 guns as the roads in the valley of the ANCRE.	
	27.		Attack continued on the right. Guns fire 56,000 rounds searching same targets as yesterday. Night firing as yesterday.	
	28.		Attack continued on the right. Guns fired 75,000 rounds searching same targets as yesterday. Numerous targets were obtained & fired on with good results. These targets were GERMANS retreating down the southern slopes of the valley towards the ANCRE. Night firing as yesterday.	
	29.		Attack by II Corps continued on our right. Guns fired 50,000 rounds searching same targets as yesterday. Much & ran through/with day. The observation obtained. Night firing on the roads in the valley of the ANCRE continued.	
	30.		Attack by II Corps continued on our right. Guns fired 40,000 rounds searching enemy same targets as yesterday, ie roads in the valley of the ANCRE & communication trenches on southern slopes of ANCRE VALLEY. Night firing on the roads in the valley of the ANCRE continued.	

118th Brigade.
39th Division.

118th BRIGADE MACHINE GUN COMPANY

OCTOBER 1 9 1 6

Vol 6

War Diary

of

118 Machine Gun Company.

for

Month of

October.

Vol 1.

Army Form C. 2118.

WAR DIARY
or
INTELLIGENCE SUMMARY.
(Erase heading not required.)

20

Place	Date	Hour	Summary of Events and Information	Remarks and references to Appendices
	Sept. Oct.			
FORT PROWSE (FRANCE; SHEET 57 D S.E. Q.21.c)	1		Night firing continued on the roads in the valley of the ANCRE to prevent present reinforcements proceeding to THIEPVAL system of trenches	
	2			
	3		The 2 sections of the 117 M.G. Coy attached to this company on the 19th Sept. were relieved by 3 guns of this company & 5 guns of the 116 M.G. Coy owing to the 116 Inf Bde taking over front of the 118 Inf Bde front.	
	4		Situation quiet. Night firing carried on as usual	
	5			
MARTINSART W.3.	6		Relieved by the 116 M.G. Coy., relief being completed by 10 am. On completion of relief, Coy moved into reserve in billets in MARTINSART (W.3.) Company reorganised.	
	7 to 9			
AUTHUILLE WOOD (W.12.b.)	10.		During the night of the 9/10th, billets were shelled, 2 men killed, + 14 wounded, in MARTINSART This company relieved the 117 M.G. Coy in the THIEPVAL SECTION, relief being completed at 7 p.m. 2 days rations were carried as the 118 Inf Bde were detailed to capture the remaining portion of the SCHWABEN REDOUBT.	

Army Form C. 2118.

21.

WAR DIARY
or
INTELLIGENCE SUMMARY.
(Erase heading not required.)

Place	Date	Hour	Summary of Events and Information	Remarks and references to Appendices
AUTHUILLE WOOD	Oct. 11 to 13			
	14		Arrangements made for the attack on the SCHWABEN REDOUBT. 5 guns were detailed to go over with the 4th wave. 2 officers were detailed to accompany these guns, + a carrying party of 5 men was attached to each gun team. Brigade attacked at 2.16 p.m. Attack was very successful + over 300 prisoners were taken. In moving up to the captured trenches 2 guns were destroyed by shell fire. These were replaced by guns (+ teams) held in reserve. The gun detachments did especially good work. 2nd Lt T.F. Cunningham on noticing that the infantry were held up at about R.19.d.9.9. rushed forward with a gun team, mounted the gun in a shell hole + opened fire on the enemy who were firing on our troops. This gun continued firing until all the team were wounded + the gun destroyed by shell fire. All 5 guns were in position by midnight.	
	15		At dawn to this morning, the enemy counter attacked, but not strongly. The machine guns did good work in repelling the enemy. Enemy heavily shelled the captured trenches, making communication + supplying very difficult.	

WAR DIARY or INTELLIGENCE SUMMARY.

Army Form C. 2118.

Place	Date	Hour	Summary of Events and Information	Remarks and references to Appendices
AUTHUILLE WOOD	Oct. 15 Contd.		The casualties during the attack & consolidation of SCHWABEN REDOUBT were 2 men killed + 3 officers + 15 O.R. wounded. The officers wounded were 2 Lt T.F. Cunningham, 2 Lt Y. Glover + 2 Lt F. Palmer. Reinforcement of 10 O.R. arrived.	
	16		12 guns remained in action. 2 had been destroyed by shell fire & 2 were being out of action owing to broken cheek-lever-plates. Enemy counter-attacked against the N.E. portion of the SCHWABEN REDOUBT. This attack was easily repulsed. The machine guns did useful work. 4 guns of this company were relieved by the 117 M.G. Coy in the left sub-section, the relief being completed by 7 p.m. The guns in SCHWABEN REDOUBT were not relieved. The remaining 8 guns in the right sub section were relieved by the 116 M.G. Coy, the relief being completed by 11 p.m. On completion of relief, the coy moved into reserve in huts in MARTINSART WOOD at W.3.C.	
MARTINSART (W.3.a.9.8.)	17		Coy rested + reorganised.	
	18 & 19			
	20		Reinforcement of 11 O.R. arrived. Also 2 Lt N.R. Crum-Ewing reported for duty from CAMIERS.	
SENLIS (V.10.d.)	21		During to enemy shelling MARTINSART, H.Q moved to SENLIS arriving at 12 noon.	

WAR DIARY
or
INTELLIGENCE SUMMARY
(Erase heading not required.)

Army Form C. 2118.
23

Place	Date	Hour	Summary of Events and Information	Remarks and references to Appendices
SENLIS (V.10d)	Oct 21 (contd.)		Coy still remained in huts in MARTINSART WOOD.	
	22		Orders received that the II Corps was to attack on the night of the river ANCRE while the V. Corps attacked on the left of the river. The 39th Div were to capture ST PIERRE DIVION (Q.24.b) & the line of the RIVER ANCRE from R.8.c.2.0 to about Q.24.8.0.0. The 118 Inf. Bde is to be the assaulting brigade.	
	23		Arrangements made for the attack	
	24		Received orders to relieve the 117 M.G. Coy in the THIEPVAL SECTION, but relief was postponed owing to operations being postponed until the 28th inst. Weather very rainy.	
	25		Lieut W. GORE, 2nd in command transferred to assume command of 51st M.G. Coy. 2nd Lt A.T.H. Hall reported from GRANTHAM for duty.	
	26		Coy moved from MARTINSART WOOD to huts in SENLIS (V.10.d). This move is due to increased activity of enemy artillery.	
	27		Operations again postponed until the 30th inst owing to heavy rain.	
	28		Lieut R. Ellrington reported for duty from the 100th M.G. Coy	
AUTHUILLE Q.36.c.3.3	29		This company relieved the 117 M.G. Coy in THIEPVAL SECTION, the relief being completed 3.30 p.m.	

Army Form C. 2118.

2/4

WAR DIARY
or
INTELLIGENCE SUMMARY.
(Erase heading not required.)

Instructions regarding War Diaries and Intelligence Summaries are contained in F.S. Regs., Part II. and the Staff Manual respectively. Title pages will be prepared in manuscript.

Place	Date	Hour	Summary of Events and Information	Remarks and references to Appendices
W.9.d.9.9.	Oct 30		Relieved by the 116 M.G. Coy, the relief being completion by 2.30 p.m. Two sections remained in the line under the command of the O.C. 116 M.G. Coy. On completion of relief, headquarters & the 2 remaining sections moved into dug-outs at W.9.d.9.9.	
	31		Very heavy rain during the afternoon. Awaiting orders. Weather has cleared up	

118th Brigade.
39th Division.

118th BRIGADE MACHINE GUN COMPANY

NOVEMBER 1 9 1 6

Confidential.

No 7

War Diary

of

118th Machine Gun Company

for the month of

November 1916

WAR DIARY or INTELLIGENCE SUMMARY

Army Form C. 2118.

25

Place	Date	Hour	Summary of Events and Information	Remarks and references to Appendices
AUTHUILLE SENLIS (Q.36.c.3.3)	Nov. 1		Relieved the 116 M.G. Coy in THIEPVAL SECTION, relief being completed at 5 p.m. The company had 2 casualties during the relief.	
	2		Ammunition carried up & arrangements made for the attack on ST PIERRE DIVION. The attack has been postponed owing to the bad weather & the impassable state of the ground.	
SENLIS (V.10.d.)	3		117 M.G. Coy relieved this company, the relief being completed by 6.30 p.m. On completion of relief, the company moved into reserve at SENLIS	
	4 5 6		Company rested & reorganised.	
	7		Operations indefinitely postponed owing to the weather.	
	8		Orders received that operations would take place at zero hour on 9th inst. Very heavy rain. Operations cancelled owing to the heavy rain + state of the ground.	
AUTHUILLE (Q.36.c.3.3)			This company relieved the 117 M.G. Coy in THE RIVER SECTION (THIEPVAL) relief being complete at 7.25 p.m.	
	9		Arrangement made with the 189 M.G. Coy (on the north of the river ANCRE) of enfilade nightly a new trench being dug by the enemy on the slope on the hill on the south of the ANCRE	

Place	Date	Hour	Summary of Events and Information	Remarks and references to Appendices
Senlis V.16.d	Nov 10		Two Sections of this Coy were relieved by two Sections of 116th M.G. Coy. (Pioneer Section) relief being completed by 8 p.m. The two sections remaining in the line then came under the orders of the G.O.C. 116 Inf. Bde.	
Pioneer Rd	11		The two sections at Senlis moved to Pioneer Rd taking over quarters vacated by the 117th Inf. Bde. The Coy sections in the line were relieved by two sections of the 117th M.G. Coy. & joined the rest of the Coy at Pioneer Rd.	
Authuille Q.36.B.3.3.	12		The Coy moved into the line Rue Sadin (THIEPVAL) taking up the Little Position. Two Teams were attached to 1/1 Herts Regt. one to 1/1 Camb. Regt. and K. 1/6 Cheshire Regt. & one to 4/5 Royal Welch. There were the only teams detailed to go over with the new unknown during the attack. Ref. of Trench Map. SP. PIERRE DIVION 1/5000 + 1/10000 MAP. Sheet 57D NE & SE. The operations referred to here are described in rather detail as to be covered by Majors. on 2 day the 19th & 39 Divs of the II Corp on 6 captured the line R21a57 - R20189 - R14c21 - R136 4 6. Mill at R13a27 & crossing at Q18&25&0. The V Corp ale to being the General line of the BEAUCOURT Rd & Serre. The main objective of the 118th Bde in the HANSA LINE from R14c21 to R136 4 6	

WAR DIARY
INTELLIGENCE SUMMARY

Place	Date	Hour	Summary of Events and Information	Remarks and references to Appendices
Contd	12		The Stokes teams & 2 L.G. teams have been moved to "Provide S.A.A. & Carriers. The teams	
		4 p.m	in the Little Positions have just been given their brew of S.A.A. sent up to Sunk 4 them.	
Paisley Dump (Thiepval)	13	5.15 AM ZERO hour.	Misty morning. 18 Pounder bombardment Commences. Sight of our guns on support of the NAVAL DIV. on the left of the ANCRE. The objective was Sameed will few losses by about 6.30 AM. All our teams with 14 except of the one with 1/6 Cheshires got over safely. This team owing to shell fire lost its Commander & went back for more.	
			In the afternoon four teams were sent forward to the HANSA LINE under Lt Brockbank L > Lt. Hall to consolidate.	
St Pierre Divion	14	2 AM	Have sent for two teams to replace Casualties. Lt Brockbank & his team having been reported knocked out by shell fire. Lt B. reported suffering from shell shock. Capt Andrews & Lt Bramah wounded while laying in Schwaben Redoubt.	
		3.30 AM	Teams have arrived under 2/Lt Lemartey & have gone up to positions in HANSA LINE. This officer carried out orders well & knew position & did good work in Causing as much	
			Teams have at work improving Positions during the day.	

Army Form C. 2118.

28

WAR DIARY
or
INTELLIGENCE SUMMARY.
(Erase heading not required.)

Instructions regarding War Diaries and Intelligence Summaries are contained in F. S. Regs., Part II. and the Staff Manual respectively. Title pages will be prepared in manuscript.

Place	Date	Hour	Summary of Events and Information	Remarks and references to Appendices
	Nov.			
St. PIERRE DIVION	15	6PM	Teams in HANSA LINE relieved by teams of 5th M.G. Coy. There is SCHWABEN. Sent out of the line without delay now out of the defence scheme.	
SENLIS WARLOY	15		The Coy to be armed in Billets here.	
WARLOY	15		The Coy moved to WARLOY. Leaving SENLIS at 2.30pm. Officers & men all very tired but place did not exceed 3 miles per hour. Everyone very cheery. Weather fine.	
R. of France Sheet 57D V/40000 AMPLIER- ORVILLE AREA	16		The Coy moved to billets in AMPLIER-ORVILLE AREA. Place did not exceed two miles per hour. Steel helmets were not worn. Billets & weather good.	
"	17		Resting & cleaning up in AMPLIER-ORVILLE AREA.	
DOULLENS & CANDAS (LENS. II. Sheet)	18		Half the Coy moved to DOULLENS & half to CANDAS. transport also slept up for purpose of entraining.	
do.	19	6.30 A.M.	Coy entrained for WORMHOUDT.	
WORMHOUDT	20		That the Coy detrained at Capt. EsquelBECK + half in POPERINGE. Marching from the Detrainment Places to WORMHOUDT. Good Billets for both Officers & men.	

WAR DIARY
INTELLIGENCE SUMMARY

Army Form C. 2118.

Place	Date	Hour	Summary of Events and Information	Remarks and references to Appendices
WORMHOUDT	20		Coy spent day cleaning Equipment etc. 9AM – 1pm. Remainder of day free	
"	21		Coy continued cleaning equipment. Also from 3-5pm Pals etc checked & allowances struck undertaken for.	
			In a special Order of the day Brigadier General E. Snot-HATTON congratulated his officers & men on the "Glorious Victory they had achieved."	
"	22		Coy see new training. Hours as from 9.AM – 1pm. Programme as follows: Red to Brigade HQ. daily. The following a.m. Infantry Programme. 9-9.30. mspecton of Rifle, Gas Helmets & Equipment. 9.30–10.15. Physical training. 10.30–11.30. Instruction in mechanism & stoppages of Lewis Gun & mountings. 11.45–12.15pm Rifle & Squad Drill Stoppages & advanced drill for trained men. 12.15t – 12.50. Lecture. Review of recent attack at worney M.S.D. The Officers men played football in the afternoon. Matches were arranged with W A.S.C. Coy was tasked to section in Town, as that work was still carried out.	
"	23		Coy trained as per Programme.	
"	24		do. Lieut sn-Gloky, from 109 Coy reported for duty a C.O.	
"	25		do. with exception of one hour devoted to Divine Service.	
"	26		The C.O. made a reconnaissance of (Ref 1/30000 Map Sheet 38 N.W.) hill from B12 a 67 to	

WAR DIARY
INTELLIGENCE SUMMARY

Army Form C. 2118.

Place	Date	Hour	Summary of Events and Information	Remarks and references to Appendices
	Cont'd			
	26		B.U.C.'s. Held by 79th FRENCH Regt. & one half of 80th FRENCH Regt. (5th BELGIAN DIV.)	
WORMHOUDT	27		Coy training as per Programme.	
CAMP F. Sh.1/20000/MAP Sheet 28. (AIC 667.)	28		Coy marched to Camp F. arriving 3.30 pm. Cooks had been sent ahead & a hot meal was provided for the men on arrival.	
B.13.b.28.	29		12 Guns of this Coy relieved the Guns of the 77th M.G. Coy in the Sector recommended by the C.O. on the 26th inst. The relief was carried out unexpectedly & without incident. Guides were met at 4.30 pm & relief was completed by 8 pm. reported to Brig "Hunter". The remaining four Guns are in Reserve posts in the vicinity of the Section Reports received during day from all Section Commanders. H.Q. Section busy all day carrying up S.A.A. Rations Greasing ammunition, overhauling wells. In hilos in the relief apparent anywhere. A French M.G. Officer reconnoitred behind to our day to clean up any doubtful points but nothing has arisen. The left has been very busy during day altering & improving the Emplacements. The Section Officers appear to have necessary alterations well in hand.	
do.	30		The C.O. & Sec in Command went round the line again visiting each position.	

F.Edmonston Lieut. for O.C. 118th Machine Gun Coy.

118th Brigade.
39th Division.

118th BRIGADE

MACHINE GUN COMPANY

DECEMBER 1 9 1 6

WAR DIARY
INTELLIGENCE SUMMARY

Army Form C. 2118 / 118 M G Coy / Feb 8 / 31

Place	Date	Hour	Summary of Events and Information	Remarks and references to Appendices
DECOUCK FARM B.13.b.2.8 Ref (Belgian) Sheet 28 N.W.	Dec 1		Coy still in the line. Sector abnormally quiet c/s SOMME. Strict orders issued in subject of cleanliness in the line.	Most/Bester
"	2		Orders issued by C.O. to set in line emphasing necessity of ready to subject? Coy will guard case. All men in line to be listed daily in by the Lewis Gun instructors with thorough officer. Reference cleanliness thinking the No complaint of not being the necessary cleaning kit. In reality but no sd. It was explained that a soldier should always find some way of keeping himself clean — tidy and in similar abilities with view of well always read in emergency to be ready in busiest battles. The trench supplements having to charge + also not suitable for our posts + Vickers in very crowded attacks. Nightly working party for posts now supplies will to have S.A.A. + 6 lett Boxes, 2 Rabbit Knives in Webley in use of Lewis posts. Work of altering implemental customs — Book M.G. lead this evening. New Crpd N. C.O. + Sec. Command in the ELVERDINGE, BOESINGHE Rds. BOESINGHE village dos reached by few MG fire. Weather still hardly	
"	3			
"	4		Three guns withdrawn from A. LINE (front line), the peace of but was taken by	

WAR DIARY / INTELLIGENCE SUMMARY

Army Form C. 2118.
32

Place	Date	Hour	Summary of Events and Information	Remarks and references to Appendices
	End of 4		Lewis Gun. A limit now of 1 MG pr line & appears now a place Lewis Gun throughout. The three Coys relieved one another.	
	5		They are being billeted in huts easily reopened by the trenches. Nothing of importance occurred during the day. The 3 teams at Coy H.Q. carried out training programme. Irwin left with Roy Rayner - made by section in Groups of 7. See 2nd Army Pamphlet on "Chilled pot portable". One has been longer advised who had not had his lot M for 7 days. No Doyen Store assembly Bde to be 1 man in Pit 9 hand Stove called for from all sections. Board in Rouge Camp moved to all teams. The CO made his daily inspection of the line & noticed considerable improvement in appearance of men. Arrangt. was made by Coy means up to standard required.	
	6		One of our Guns fired 750 Rds on Enemy travel Tramway trench & Roads passing N.E thereof. C.i.c & C.i.d. (Maturity 28.N.W.2. ST JULIEN) weather continues fine but misty	
	7		Section relief carried out. 3 teams from Coy H.Q. & the line from Coy.	

INTELLIGENCE SUMMARY

(Erase heading not required.)

Place	Date	Hour	Summary of Events and Information	Remarks and references to Appendices
	Cont'd			
"	7		relieved 4 teams in 'L' defence. These four teams relieved 3 teams in B LINE & occupied the the Emplacements vacated by the relieved teams in C line. The difficulty of relief with no teams in reserve at, was overcome by sending in teams in reference to N.C.E. reference to C team as t relieved the teams there which proceeded to teams in reserve to 'M'. He other two teams from Coy H.Q. to complete the relief. The 3 teams from 'B' line moved to Coy H.Q. as reserve	
"	8		Relief was carried out by night (moonlight) Work of improving trenches & Emplacements continued. The position in 'A' line is very much spread thing. This position is about 3070 from the general line, & is constructed of the trench width being too easily spotted on an air photograph. Suka side is also being effectively smaller. the trench wall the night. on R.E. & Tramway in German lines C 2 a 33. (R/26 N & No 2) 1000 Rounds were fired during	
"	9		Reports received that enemy working Improvement carried on	

T2134. Wt. W708—776. 500000. 4/15. Sir J. C. & S.

WAR DIARY
or
INTELLIGENCE SUMMARY

(Erase heading not required.)

Place	Date	Hour	Summary of Events and Information	Remarks and references to Appendices
DEEOUCK FARM.	10		ENEMY Shells, acted in our sector the afternoon, working improving old system in we fired 500 rounds on Pot Shannon Bd at 6 O'Clock. The men in A line	
	11.		report that they have not heard hostility using the mornings for entrenching as work of altering emplacements almost complete. French either sides improved, hung pulled down, o built a parable without altering the top plate, to shorten revetting in progress. See fired Soens. on Road & French Sos. c.13.	
"S" CAMP	12.		The Coy. have relieved by the 115th S.Cy. & moved to S' camp. Relief took place in daylight night. Was completed by 11p.m., weather changed again	
"	13		Coy. paraded 9.30am for the inspection & arms cleaning, duties of R.C.t. & spare Rest afternoon made. weather fine	
	14.		Coy paraded 9am for instruction & M.S. work, sgn cleaning.	
	15.		Regular Training Programme commenced. 7th Coy order to allow though training & too hour improvement Bath.	
	16		Bath parade for Coy. after in deserted to football.	
	17		Training Programme carried out in full. Voluntary Funeral Church in Evening under Adj Gaulin. The Rev. Kuttercroft. abt 30 O.R.anps present.	

WAR DIARY
or
INTELLIGENCE SUMMARY.
(Erase heading not required.)

Place	Date	Hour	Summary of Events and Information	Remarks and references to Appendices
S. CAMP	18.		Rehearsal Parade by Bde Commander. An extemporized inspection by G.O.C. in C. Fault noted in march past, was that men were slow in responding to the Command of "Eyes left". The men were well turned out & very clean.	
	19		Inspection by G.O.C. in C. Proposed visit having programme carried out scrap of afternoon. Permission granted to play football then. March all men out for exercise afterwards.	
	20		Manual training & improvement of Billets. All drains in Camp have been cleaned & deepened to a better flow obtained. 30 new trench boards laid down in mud nearest places.	
	21		Parade at 9 am for Inspection & drill by the C.O. before having D.N. Inspection by G.O.C. in chief. Then made away to the G.O.C. in chief who took no notice but seemed to get the order to march to the hook, so we loved lives, he inspected in Billet. Weather very bad.	
	22.		Reconnaissance of lines made in Sacks transported by 116th M.S.G., YPRES SALIENT. Thirty positions on [W a]'s Hill in clay, a under enemy observation	

INTELLIGENCE SUMMARY.

(Erase heading not required.)

Place	Date	Hour	Summary of Events and Information	Remarks and references to Appendices
C.25 CANAL BK	23		Relieved the 11th M.G. Coy in YPRES SALIENT, Commenced at 5pm & was completed by 10.30pm. There was no hitch in the relief. Zeven katen taken up. The occupy 13 positions, the remaining 3 (one at G.H.Q. CANAL BK. Headqtrs and 2 filled wells taken over at Sout Poston. Bay 3 MENT & NCO. Bompue or gun teams, only is each of Coronoeskin.	
"	24		Working Parties sent up to various Positions in the lines, all the Postns are badly constructed, though he held & for in short little or no Protection for the Summer or team. All emplacements being rebuilt & he hands channel & walls of Trenches revetted. Strictest orders reissued regard Trench feet & prevention of same. Also a reminder sent re Gas attacks. Orders issued that Bombardment drill must take place daily.	
	25		Improvements to emplacements were carried on, also having of trench near B.13. One artillery was active throughout the day, especially about 9.30 p.m., when there was also heavy shelling of left subsection by the enemy. A printed extromation message from the Corps Commander was distributed to all ranks.	

WAR DIARY
or
INTELLIGENCE SUMMARY.
(Erase heading not required.)

Army Form C. 2118.
34

Place	Date	Hour	Summary of Events and Information	Remarks and references to Appendices
	26		A working party was sent up to work on emplacements in Ruyulx subsection. Emplacement at B.13 was relieved. Christmas message to the troop received from H.H The King	
	27 28		A quiet day in this front; section commanders had instructions to report. Nothing of importance reported. Enemy artillery fire normal.	
	29		Usual work of improving emplacements carried out. Hostile artillery active on right battalion front.	
	30		Hostile artillery more active. Enemy M.G. fire on chequerboard trench. Heavy raining considerably damaged trenches. Several any mine galleries through the same. Unusual fire	
	30		of shell reported near trenches, when a 4.5" or 5.9" came. Blight explosion in back the woods about 400 yds to front. Seen again in percussion with loud detonals.	
	31		Hostile artillery have active than usual. Trenches in vicinity on improved being repaired. But were apparently taken in increased interest in their several experiences & in the work of improvement of emplacements.	

G.R. Wainwright Lt Col
Cmdg 3rd Bn 11th Inf

Army Form C. 2118.

118 M.G. Coy
38
July 9

WAR DIARY
or
INTELLIGENCE SUMMARY.
(Erase heading not required.)

Place	Date	Hour	Summary of Events and Information	Remarks and references to Appendices
CANAL BK. C.25.d.8.w. SHEET. 28NW EDIT. 3.E	February 1		Enemy Artillery registered on our front line. Booche Captured 4 others. Carried by Lewis Gun fire. Our M.G. did not open fire, though were ready for any development. Our Artillery replied vigorously to the Booche barrage.	
	2		Usual work carried out. Enemy morning hate Crucifix for several hours on BUNDEY Ra. & BENT.Ra C.26.d.7.v. Sheet 50* in front of WILSON Fm. is of what was termed.	
	3		Emplacement of WILSON Fm. revetted. All guns ready in anticipation of another raid. ENEMY M.G. location spotted on Gun at C.21.a.8.p.	
	4		Questioning - Two Booche Aeroplanes on our lines in the afternoon. Heavy gun fire on 4 M.G.'s G's on right (166). Held M.G. posters on BENT Rd.	
	5		Enemy Artillery fairly quiet throughout the day. Telephone overhead very line all night 10 Am - Half of their force in need on our lines 6.30 night. C..... for the morning. Enemy working improving to have carried out short bound neutralized to position.	

WAR DIARY or INTELLIGENCE SUMMARY

Army Form C. 2118.
39

Place	Date	Hour	Summary of Events and Information	Remarks and references to Appendices
	6		Troops posted at B13 Postn. Down billets (in 38 hrs) No troops at B13 Stn dugouts. 1/8 Oxfords holding the billets not relieved by 1/6 Hampshire. Quiet day. Bill me, with one seed, fell into 4 in Parados in Trench. Stormy. Evening quiet. Enemy has in B16 Postn.	
	6½			
	7		Quiet day. Enemy tanner line overlooking B13 slightly. One from at B16 to W.Loo FM. fired on NO MANS LAND. St shell of shyb part slew near CLIFFORD Trench. Knocked out the Jm at hot lode, Parcel stopped by shrap. 8 pratspd terminyn b Brench coy in coppist B36 fallen. Quiet again. 8pm relieved inf. in by 1/8 Warwick, got into new line. About 11.30 pm. very wet. When way over it however, parados slew on line, to mends. cod protested up.	
	8		Quiet day. Changes round at all Postns. All reinspected. Enemy put several heavy shells into YPRES. his M.G. not working as usual.	
	9		Our Arty. sent a few shells with HE stopped. Sentry for fretel. Enemy dropped later to myself HAMPSHIRE Reg.	

WAR DIARY

INTELLIGENCE SUMMARY

Army Form C. 2118.
40

Place	Date	Hour	Summary of Events and Information	Remarks and references to Appendices
	9		All feet inspected.	
	10		Bn. 12.0 – 12.30 Army Commander & 5.9" shells landed on HILLTOP, our team in parts shot to nothing doing. Heavy artillery fire put into a afternoon. Hostile shrapnel in Evening. Day went fairly quiet. Fully up ind & 5 Div in on nightline. Ever went Sunday dept. fully up & red + Green double lights.	
			All feet inspected. Turned down & too caused us.	
	11		Quiet day in the seats. Craftsman casualties j/. Lt/. Herbert Sayer of BRAND, Lieut 4. 7. S.C.M. 5 Pr Crump hear Sec 4 @ 7 A.M. pm met fire from S.M. (B10) on right 1/4/12 during enemy raid. This Son Lieut g his officer to use Pistols to fire to the duration land (where 6 Lt 30 05 went up in Enemy trenches on front) of the Lot 305 went up in Enemy trenches on front, little happened.	
	12		Officers D. 118, M.S. G, Animals 4, 63 road fire in trenches. Lt Kolby into in 12". He VIII Corp. Commander visited our Every Post 30 Yards in HILLTOP + Year Fry. Run down + int in View & from M So Baly in Evening All feet inspected. Sgt BOND transferred	

WAR DIARY
INTELLIGENCE SUMMARY

Army Form C. 2118.

Place	Date	Hour	Summary of Events and Information	Remarks and references to Appendices
	12		Relieved 6a North & 18 North comp with H.L. Batt'n to 18 North comp with H.L. now held by Bde Commander. Scheme promulgated by Corps & sent to Company. Capt. Cloke, C.O. proceeded on 10 days leave to IRELAND.	
			S.O.S signals tried out by telephoning two Corps First, Second, Third & in L.G. open & fire immediately commenced with 10en(?) of our Artillery with 1.Y.S. & Col on terms most(?) & to shortest plane.	
	13		A wet morning, heavy rain, patches of sunshine on return in afternoon. Spell in position quiet, to S.O. Sub Sector relieved by BOUNDREY Rd. Consolidation of old wire to the HUN system are (uncompleted?)	
	14		HM 8 Coy relieves the C.Coy. HQ C.Coy moved to Dug. out at LEFT SEC'N of MT Dug out front WELTJE BARN HALLEBAST 13 June & the M & S.Coy in line to gd. with C, H.Q. est.	
	15		Enemy artillery unusually active for most of the day, doing considerable damage to parts of the line. POTIZE & STEFAN shelled for first	

WAR DIARY
or
INTELLIGENCE SUMMARY

Army Form C. 2118.

Place	Date	Hour	Summary of Events and Information	Remarks and references to Appendices
	16		time for a long period. Pte. DAVIDSON departed morning, his body was received under debris by a party repairing trenches. 2/Lt. HANKS returned from a course at CAMIERS. Very quiet day in the line. Usual routine work and improvement of emplacements carried out. The team occupying LA BRIQUE was relieved by a team of 1/14th M.G. Coy, going in a reserve of 4 guns at Coy. Hd Q.	
	17.		A daylight room to lette established at ST. JEAN and 50 pairs of such sent up to night firing and day firing carried out by 1 mm at A.5 + C.27.5. according to a daily programme. Reported from WIELTJE that activity could be seen snowballing. Quiet day. Very cold + snowing. Germans could be seen snowballing. Reinforcements of O/R arrived of whom 3 are new men from CURRTIN'S with 10 weeks training on the Guns.	
	18		Cold weather continues. Snow lying & falling at intervals. A quiet day. 3 O/R, strained sinews, reported in turn for 1/1 CAMPS.	
	19		Snow still lying. Brigade Commander visited teams at WIELTJE & expressed his satisfaction with them & the emplacements that	

WAR DIARY
or
INTELLIGENCE SUMMARY
(Erase heading not required.)

Army Form C. 2118.

Place	Date	Hour	Summary of Events and Information	Remarks and references to Appendices
	20		Hostile shelling in the vicinity of Coy. H.Q. with shrapnel & H.E. continued from 12.30 to 3.15 p.m. 170 shells fired. O.C. 117th M.G.C. arrived & went round the positions on reconnaissance. Frost continues. Dull, visibility poor. Men at Coy. H.Q. working on improvement of billets. Quiet day in the line. Lt. ODOM & an officer of 1/1 CAMBS reconnoitred ARGYLE FARM. Simultaneously 2 Germans making some reconnaissance were captured by Lewis gun post. 2 teams WIELTJE section relieved.	
	21		Hard frost. Slight shelling and much machine gun fire on our front. Nothing of importance occurred.	
	22		Hard frost. Bright day, and aeroplanes again busy.	
	23		Clear frosty day. A great number of airfights took place. One of ours at WIELTJE & POTIJZE fired on aeroplane.	
	24		Capt. CLOREY O.C. returned from leave. Relief of the Company by 17th M.G. Coy. 9 & 10 am guns taking over the defensive positions in YPRES under Lt. ODOM & 2nd Lt. HANKS. Remainder of Company moved to BRANDHOEK	

Army Form C. 2118.

WAR DIARY
or
INTELLIGENCE SUMMARY

(Erase heading not required.)

Place	Date	Hour	Summary of Events and Information	Remarks and references to Appendices
BRANDHOEK	Jan. 25th		to B. Camp (No.10). Relieved teams reached camp 2 a.m. men cleaning guns + equipment. Programme of work sent in to Corps. M.G. Officer for 7 days.	
	Jan 26th		Lt. ELLERINGTON 2nd in Command went on leave to ENGLAND. Anti-aircraft shell fell in transport lines POPERINGHE killing 1 mule + wounding 1 horse and 10 mules belonging to the Company, as well as several animals belonging to BLACK WATCH.	
	Jan 27th		Training programme carried out; inspection of the Section in reserve trenches. Lt. ODOM 2/Lt CRANLEY + 6 N.C.Os attended a course for identification of hostile aeroplanes.	
	Jan 28th		Wrote intending to programme, also Divine Service. The half company in rest had their Christmas dinner in the evening, this being the first opportunity.	
	Jan 29th		Relief carried out of the 9 teams in the YPRES defences.	
	Jan 30th		Teams returned cleaning equipment. Baths at POPERINGHE + Kit inspection.	
	Jan 31st		Training programme carried out.	

[signature] Captain commanding 9 Coy to 05/16

Army Form C. 2118.

WAR DIARY
or
INTELLIGENCE SUMMARY.
(Erase heading not required.)

Army Form C. 2118.

118th Obee. Jun. Coy

Place	Date	Hour	Summary of Events and Information	Remarks and references to Appendices
	1917			
BRANDHOEK	Feb. 1st		Training programme carried out. Half Company in Rest inspected by M.O. for Scabies & Stomatitis. O.C. & Lieut. C.R.V.N. EWING went to 117th In. 9. Coy. H.Q. at DEADEND to arrange relief. Severe bombardment reported from the YPRES defences. About 2,000 shells sent over apparently with the object of knocking out R.A. batteries. In 9 stripped electrical filum 25 yds away. Nothing of interest to record on this day.	
	Feb 2nd			
	Feb 3rd		Preparing for relief of 117th In 9 Coy in the WIELTJE sector. At 11.10 a.m. Telegram received ordering Company to parade in full marching order with First line Transport packed. Marquee was sent by cyclist to Transport lines, starting 11.20 a.m. All packed up & ready to put on transport by 12.30 p.m. Transport arrived 1.20 p.m. Orders were then received to discontinue task. Relief carried out; No 3 Section forming YPRES defences to ST. JEAN, 1 & 4 from YPRES defences to reserve at Coy H.Q.	

T2134. Wt. W708—776. 500000. 4/15. Sir J. C. & S.

Army Form C. 2118.

No. ....
DATE 46
MACHINE COY

WAR DIARY
or
INTELLIGENCE SUMMARY.
(Erase heading not required.)

Instructions regarding War Diaries and Intelligence Summaries are contained in F. S. Regs, Part II. and the Staff Manual respectively. Title pages will be prepared in manuscript.

Place	Date	Hour	Summary of Events and Information	Remarks and references to Appendices
	Feb 4th		Position vacated by team were but taken over by 116 a.m. 9 Coy until next day. No. 2 Section marched from BRANDHOEK at 4.30 p.m. & went into WIELTJE subsector ; No. 1 Section from BRANDHOEK & POTIJZE subsectors. Relief complete 11.30 p.m.	
	Feb 5th		Exceptionally quiet on our front during the night 3rd/4th & throughout the day. Another very quiet day. A few whizzbangs & C 28.3 and a few bursts in MANMOUTH Tr. and exchange of shells late in the afternoon opposite WIELTJE represents the only activity. Enemy were repairing their trenches at CAMBRAI TRENCH.	
	Feb 6th		The Divisional Machine Gun Officer went round the positions on inspection duty. Our artillery very active in the afternoon & bro- -ucemed activity of hostile artillery especially about ST JEAN during the night 5/6th. Night fairly quiet & no work by	

T2134. Wt. W708—776. 500000. 4/15. Sir J. C. & S.

WAR DIARY
or
INTELLIGENCE SUMMARY.
(Erase heading not required.)

Army Form C. 2118.

Place	Date	Hour	Summary of Events and Information	Remarks and references to Appendices
	Feb 7th		guns at C27.4 & C27.5 Enemy tried to break about O.BENG F.2 & DIVIDE F.3 + RAT FM	
	Feb 8th		Frost continues. Enemy artillery active during the day in the direction of POTIZE & also HILLTOP. Night firing of guns at C27.4 & C27.5 carried out on the same targets as before. Lt. ELLERINGTON reported back from leave. Our artillery began series of bombardments according to programme. Intense bombardment 8.30 – 8.40 p.m. Enemy retaliation not very important. Night found us unmolested by his guns. One gun damaged sent to 24DAC	
	Feb 9th		Bombardment by our artillery continued according to programme at night, in addition to the two guns usually firing, two more were detailed, one in MINCEMEAT R & one in CONGREVE WALK, to fire on enemy wire & points known as opposite it. – Intense fire of artillery 9.30 – 9.40 p.m. which we find paid Enemy reply very prompt & vigorous. Later, enemy had trouble, his own front line apparently with the idea that they had been missed	

T2134. Wt. W708—776. 500000. 4/15. Sir J. C. & S.

WAR DIARY or INTELLIGENCE SUMMARY

Army Form C. 2118.

No. 118th
4 8

Place	Date	Hour	Summary of Events and Information	Remarks and references to Appendices
	Feb	10th	Bombardment continued according to programme. Enemy artillery also very active especially towards evening. Intense bombardment times to 9.5 - 9.15 p.m. took place 15 minutes earlier, enemy reply into a barrage after an interval. Form of our fire by our fired, hoped into & after an intensive barrage 5000 rounds fired. Our trench in front line was hit & damaged by shell fire. Craphead elevating screw destroyed, into gun was able to continue.	
	Feb	11th	Our artillery carried out Drill Barrage 2.30 - 2.40 p.m. One of our aeroplanes flew along the front line very low observing effect of fire. The enemy replied vigorously on POTIJZE & ST. JEAN road. Lt. GIBBIN & 116 to B Coy. arrived to reinforce with O.C. party to reconnaissance to be from Feb 12th. 10.30 p.m. our artillery again carried out a Drill Barrage. Reply came in 3½ minutes after 2 quite violent vollies but front to front KAISER BILL & one from heavy bty CAMBRAI STR & CAMBRAI SUPPORT	

WAR DIARY
or
INTELLIGENCE SUMMARY.

Army Form C. 2118.

Place	Date	Hour	Summary of Events and Information	Remarks and references to Appendices

Our guns at C.27.d. & C.27.c fired in answer from 6 till 10.30 p.m and again opened simultaneously into the artillery at 10.30 p.m continuing till midnight firing on CAMBRAI DRIVE + on Road Rectine Jct. C.23.c.97-65.

Two other guns fired throughout the night on the enemy's wire total rounds fired by all guns 65000. One gun opened fire on a fine target about 500 yds behind enemy line in direction of VON HUGEL F.7 at 6.15 p.m.

Feb. 12. Lt. GIBBON & 3 gun team & convoy of 116th M.G. Coy arrived 3.30 a.m. & took the guns up to POTIJZE, returning to Coy HQ to await the night.

Outside a carrying party taking up belt boxes to ST-JEAN came under shell fire and Pte WEBSTER & Pte WILCOX were wounded + sent to Field Ambulance

Artillery Drill Barrage from 8.15 till 6.25 a.m. Enemy did not reply.

Army Form C. 2118.

WAR DIARY
or
INTELLIGENCE SUMMARY.
(Erase heading not required.)

Instructions regarding War Diaries and Intelligence Summaries are contained in F. S. Regs., Part II. and the Staff Manual respectively. Title pages will be prepared in manuscript.

Place	Date	Hour	Summary of Events and Information	Remarks and references to Appendices
			At zero hour for the raid arranged for this night was 11.15 p.m. At Zero – 4 minutes Artillery barrage started together with firing of our guns + 3 of 1/1 116 to Company. All tore (?) was fired according to arrangements on the trenches + tracks in rear + flank of the areas to be raided. 60 men of the 1/1 HERTS. went over at 11.15 p.m. + returned at 11.35 hrs. + having 2 prisoners + reporting several found killed. Casualties in the raiding party were slight + none killed. Enemy replied 2½ minutes after barrage opened, but very soon stopped, even before the raiders returned. Two of our guns fired before Zero + went on to enclose the house + shortly + continued to fire for 1 hour after the raiders returned. A very successful affair for all concerned.	
	Feb. 13th		Thawing. R.E. started repairs to COY H.Q. Enemy Artillery very active all day, especially Canals screen. A battery dump was SALVATION CORNER blown up. A H.V. gun enfilading the road at ST JEAN.	

WAR DIARY
or
INTELLIGENCE SUMMARY
(Erase heading not required.)

Army Form C. 2118.

No. 51

Place	Date	Hour	Summary of Events and Information	Remarks and references to Appendices
	14		2/Lt. CRAWLEY & 3 teams relieved Lt. ODOM M.C. & his teams at WIELTJE. 2/Lt. THOMAS relieved 2/Lt. HALL at POTIJZE. 2/Lt. CUTTS relieved by 2/Lt. HALL at ST. JEAN. Teams at WIELTJE F.W. relieved by a team of No.3 section at 12.30 a.m. raid by 117th Infantry Brigade on the right Brigade Front, covered by artillery & machine gun barrage.	
	15		Thawing. Hostile artillery normal. Ten of our aeroplanes attacked by 5 Boche machines. Our force to retreat. One of our machines commenced fire for some time. Indirect fire for unseen indirect targets. Except for vigorous M.G. fire from an A.A M. gun on M.G. fired at night, on line road indicated for targets. Hostile artillery active. Refuelled from ST. JEAN.–POTIJZE line & YPRES. ST. JEAN shelled by H.V. guns in vicinity of R.E. dump. Accompany to very large & lower appears to be easily recognised by enemy airmen on M.G. fired on the stored targets.	
	16		Prepared for relief by 146th M.S.C.y. Trench stores checked & listed ready for handing over. Comparatively quiet day. On M.S.g. fired on the usual targets.	

WAR DIARY
or
INTELLIGENCE SUMMARY.

Army Form C. 2118.

Place	Date	Hour	Summary of Events and Information	Remarks and references to Appendices
S. Camp.	17		The Coy was relieved by 166th M.G.Coy. The C.O. arrived early in the day to talk over any points which had been shortened since he was last in the Sector. The Coy arrived afs. dark by train to YPRES. on relief 2½ sections of the Coy marched to S. CAMP. ½ section & ½ section by train to ABEELE & A.A. duty. Coy just being late to Man the Barrage morning there.	
Y. Camp.	18		Coy moved to Y. CAMP. (nr POPERINGE - WATOU Rd) morning 1½ Section on duty at ABEELE. Accomodation for men very good.	
	19		Both days spent cleaning up. Checking Shore Kent & mainly	
	20		Kit etc. Programme of work for 21st Sent to Bde H.Q. & 3 Dvl. Coy batted in 29½	
	21		Training Programme carried out from 9A.M. - 1P.M. - 2.15P.M. - 4P.M. Lecture turning etc. 5P.M. - 5.30P.M. Baths.	
	22		Training Programme carried out as for 21st. Above order drill & Physical drill form Part of the Programme. M.G. drill, mechanism & Tips &c & lecture constitute in my reading & instruct per Sec. jolly.	
	23		The remainder of Programme training Programme carried out as usual.	

WAR DIARY or INTELLIGENCE SUMMARY.

Army Form C. 2118.

(Erase heading not required.)

Place	Date	Hour	Summary of Events and Information	Remarks and references to Appendices
	24		Usual training programme carried out. The all melancholy comment "2 cases of scabies found". When I the Coy were mustered on the parade less than 1/2 came up for this & other diseases.	
	25		Usual training programme carried out. The all day known the afternoon game.	
	26		Usual programme carried out. F's section attended at Y camp for ABEELE. Coy from 9 to 3.30 pm Remrs preparing to move on 27th. Bn Shrapnel has to move to Scherp on 27th to ERIE Camp F11.C.6.4. with 6th then transpt of Bde.inde. Bde T.O.	
ERIE Camp F11.C.6.4	27		Coy left Y Camp at 8.15 AM. Transport in rear I, 1/6 Cheshire Regt to ERIE Camp.	
	28		Training Programme carried out as usual. Programme Army set 6 Bde for 28th. Good heavy food stuffs Camp, also make food for the funnel. YMCA club by the passons & which have already made friends with our men.	

P.A. Leveryton Lt.
O.C. 118th M.T.Coy.

Army Form C. 2118.

WAR DIARY
or
INTELLIGENCE SUMMARY

(Erase heading not required.)

Vol XI

CONFIDENTIAL

War Diary
of
118th Machine Gun Company.

From 1st March, 1917 To 31st March, 1917.

(Volume ~ I)

S.H. Coles Capt.
Cmdg. 118th Machine Gun Coy.

Army Form C. 2118.
112TH
No. 34
DATE
MACHINE GUN COY

WAR DIARY
or
INTELLIGENCE SUMMARY.
(Erase heading not required.)

Army Form C. 2118.

Instructions regarding War Diaries and Intelligence Summaries are contained in F. S. Regs., Part II. and the Staff Manual respectively. Title pages will be prepared in manuscript.

Place	Date	Hour	Summary of Events and Information	Remarks and references to Appendices
ERIE CAMP (G.11.c.6.2)	1st MARCH 1917		Training programme carried out. Lt ELLERINGTON and Lt ODOM M.C. went up to reconnoitre the OBSERVATORY RIDGE sector. In the afternoon the Company played the 118th T.M. Batt. at football & drew 0 all. A concert was held by the Company at 7.30 p.m. in Y.M.C.A. hut.	Ref map BELGIUM 28 NW 1/20000
	2nd		Company paraded at 8.30 a.m in full marching order & marched to TORONTO CAMP where it was inspected together with 1/6 CHESHIRES & 1/1 HERTS & 118th T.M. Batt. by G.O.C. Xth CORPS at 10 a.m. The G.O.C. Xth CORPS expressed to G.O.C. Bde his satisfaction with the clean & tidy appearance of the Company on parade. In the evening 1 M.G.O. & 2 men for each of 12 teams went up to go into the new gun positions at OBSERVATORY RIDGE sector.	
	3rd		Preparing for going into the line. C.O. went up at noon. Rest of Coy left at 5.30 p.m. entrained at BRANDHOEK to detrained at ASYLUM YPRES at 6.45 p.m. marched to LILLE GATE where guns & men were picked up from transport. Located in trenches & billets & Coy H.Q. at ZILLEBEKE BUND, where the 116th M.G. Coy was relieved. Considerable delay was caused	

Army Form C. 2118.

118TH
No. ....
DATE ....
MACHINE GUN

WAR DIARY
or
INTELLIGENCE SUMMARY.
(Erase heading not required.)

Instructions regarding War Diaries and Intelligence Summaries are contained in F.S. Regs., Part II. and the Staff Manual respectively. Title pages will be prepared in manuscript.

Place	Date	Hour	Summary of Events and Information	Remarks and references to Appendices
	1917 MARCH			
			owing to the Infantry relieving at the same time. Relief complete about 12 midnight.	
ZILLEBEKE BUND	4th		A quiet day except for hostile shelling of YPRES about 6 – 7 p.m. At 2.15 p.m. a GERMAN aeroplane came down in our lines about I 22. d.5.1., the tail falling separately near HELL BLAST Corner. The machine was probably a ALBATROSS. Enemy opened fire on it almost immediately & obtained 2 direct hits, 2 other GERMAN planes were seen to turn back. At 2.30 p.m. a small red hyper balloon flew over Cer. H.Q. from the GERMAN lines to fell about 400 yds beyond. It was secured & sent to Brigade Intelligence. Often by the Company.	
	5th		Snow fell in the night & remained on the ground throughout the day, which was quiet with few incidents.	
	6th		Very cold weather with snow showers. Again a quiet day. During the morning several minenwerfer shells were observed near No.1 Position but no damage was caused. In the afternoon visibility	

Army Form C. 2118.

No. ....
DATE ....

MACHINE GUN

WAR DIARY
INTELLIGENCE SUMMARY

(Erase heading not required.)

Instructions regarding War Diaries and Intelligence Summaries are contained in F. S. Regs., Part II. and the Staff Manual respectively. Title pages will be prepared in manuscript.

Place	Date 1917	Hour	Summary of Events and Information	Remarks and references to Appendices
ZILLEBEKE BUND (OBSERVATORY RIDGE SECTION)	MARCH 7th		Was fine and there was considerable aerial activity. Another very quiet day. During the day there was intermittent shelling close to No 1 position by minenwerfers. A dog came over from the GERMAN lines to our post in METROPOLITAN LEFT, but escaped in the afternoon & returned to his lines. A few whizz bangs during the noon near the BUND	
	8th		A quiet day with no activity reported from any of our positions. The Company was relieved by the 116th 19. G. Coy. in the OBSERVATORY RIDGE Section (Right Brigade) & relieved the 117th M.G.Cy. in the Left Brigade Sector. The relief went off well & the double move was completed by 11.30 p.m. No 1 Section was 19th Reserve at Coy H.Q. in YPRES, No 4 Section in Reserve at ZILLEBEKE BUND, No. 2 Section plus 1 gun of No.1 Section in Right Subsector, No.3 Section in Left Subsector	
YPRES (HOOGE SECTION)	9th		One section of 117th M.G. Cy. remained behind to carry on R.E. work at GORDON Hse. A quiet day in our front. About 7 p.m. a move went up to the	

Army Form C. 2118.

118TH No. 5 DATE
MACHINE GUN

WAR DIARY
INTELLIGENCE SUMMARY
(Erase heading not required.)

Place	Date 1917	Hour	Summary of Events and Information	Remarks and references to Appendices
YPRES (HOOGE SECTION)	MARCH 9th (cont'd)		Left of HOOGE. About 10 minutes later an S.O.S. signal went up & the artillery opened fire. One M.G. in CHINA WALL position also opened, but ceased in a double green light going up soon after. Artillery also ceased. Enemy aeroplanes active in the morning & at 10.30 a.m. our RITZ ST. gun fired in a hostile plane which turned away. A working party doing continuing work in dugouts of 4 men & 1 N.C.O. was provided by No. 1 & 4 Section from 12 noon to work under R.E. at new M.G. position at GORDON H⁰. Also two reliefs of 8 men supplied by No. 4 Section to 118th T.M. Batt. worked under R.E. on M.G. Soph.	
	10th		Nothing of importance reported from the line, as occurring on our front. At 6.30 p.m. the enemy blew a mine in the direction of HOOGE. The shock was accompanied by the sound of two being repeated & falling supporting that the explosion seemed in a work. 2/Lt CUTTS returned from a course of Anti Aircraft instruction with G Battery A.A. & went to the Left Section.	

T2134. Wt. W708–776. 500000. 4/15. Sir J. C. & S.

Army Form C. 2118.

No. 118TH

WAR DIARY
or
INTELLIGENCE SUMMARY.
(Erase heading not required.)

Place	Date	Hour	Summary of Events and Information	Remarks and references to Appendices
YPRES (HOOGE SECTION)	1917 March 11th		A few light shells on WELLINGTON CRESCENT and VINCE ST. near DORMY HOUSE reported. Aerial activity marked throughout the day. At 11 a.m. a hostile machine & great speed attacked & brought down in a shattered condition two of our Artillery Observation Balloons aeroplane, one of which fell in the marsh near MENIN GATE & the other near POTIJZE. The hostile plane appeared within 50 yds. of our machines & poured machine gun fire into them. During the afternoon desultory shelling of YPRES with 5.9 shell continued. The shelling became very heavy between 8 & 9 p.m. The C.O. went all round the line in the morning with the Brigade Commander & Staff Captain, who were pleased with the clean turn out & all the men of the Company whom they encountered.	
	12th		Mud & damp with occasional fine rain. Work done at Coy HTR in the erection of 2/Lt CRAWLEY & 2/Lt HANKS & clearing up of Ypres. ZILLEBEKE was shelled with 5.9s on "elephant" for use at Ypres. ZILLEBEKE was shelled with 5.9s in the afternoon. There was considerable shelling of YPRES during the	

Army Form C. 2118.

112TH

No ....
DATE ....5.J......

MACHINE GUN

WAR DIARY
or
INTELLIGENCE SUMMARY.
(Erase heading not required.)

Instructions regarding War Diaries and Intelligence Summaries are contained in F. S. Regs., Part II. and the Staff Manual respectively. Title pages will be prepared in manuscript.

Place	Date	Hour	Summary of Events and Information	Remarks and references to Appendices
YPRES (HOOGE SECTION)	MARCH 12 1917		(cont.) early part of the day which ceased altogether towards evening. Reported at 11 p.m. that FROM FORT position was unsuitable for enemy to flankers. 10 mules sent up from BUND with dry belts & to assist in taking out Gun team of mounted at Section H.Q. in WELLINGTON CRESCENT with elevation in the GAP. C.O. made his daily inspection of line. Sgt. BIRKENHEAD absent sick since Nov 11th 1916 reported back for duty, also L/C HAMLETT from Field Ambulance.	
	13th		C.O. went round the line with D.M.G.O. in morning. The enemy shelled DORMY Ho. at 2.15 p.m. with 4.2 shells. One direct hit was obtained on m.g. dugout entrance burying Pte LEACH who was extricated unwounded but shaken. About 4.45 p.m. a few 5.9 shells were dropped at 2 points along MENIN RD — H.H. FIRE CORNER & I.II.c.40.75. On nested activity was reported at dawn in this sap running from front line towards MENIN RD & the CULVERT, probably to the right of the Crater of the mine recently blown. A number of men seen entering Annex of S O/R at ERIE CAMP reported. Orders of relief received	

T2134. Wt. W708—776. 500000. 4/15. Sir J. C. & S.

Army Form C. 2118.

No. 60
DATE
MACHINE GUN
Remarks and references to Appendices

118TH

WAR DIARY

INTELLIGENCE SUMMARY.

(Erase heading not required.)

Instructions regarding War Diaries and Intelligence Summaries are contained in F. S. Regs., Part II. and the Staff Manual respectively. Title pages will be prepared in manuscript.

Place	Date	Hour	Summary of Events and Information
YPRES (HOOGE SECTION)	MARCH 1917 14th		History of importance to record. at 4.30 p.m. the relief was carried out to 117th Coy. having been recently inoculated. Very heavy shelling on MENIN GATE & LILLE GATE & between these points with 5.9., 4.7, 77 m.m. Shrapnel & gasshells especially between 6.30 and 8.30 p.m. Shelling eased about 9 p.m.
	15th		Heavy shelling of ZILLEBEKE. One casualty wounded Pte GUYER at ZILLEBEKE. Slow shelling throughout morning & afternoon of YPRES. Relieved by 117th the company moved out to ERIE CAMP, first party arriving 12.20 midnight, and last party 3 a.m.
ERIE CAMP (G11C 6.2)	16th		Inspection & cleaning of kits & accessories by action officers. 11.30 a.m. Training programme carried out including inoculation in GERMAN BELGIUM 28 NW 1/20000 machine gun. Afternoon: Football. Second team T A B second
	17th		out to a part of the Company by M.O. 1/1 HERTS. Inspection of Camp by Divisional opposite Sanitary Officer. Some more men inoculated. Training Programme drawn up, to then
	18th		day (Sunday) cancelled by Brigade. Inspection of Transport by

Army Form C. 2118.

WAR DIARY
or
INTELLIGENCE SUMMARY

(Erase heading not required.)

No. 118TH 61
MACHINE GUN Coy

Ref map
BELGIUM
28 NW
1-20000

Place	Date 1917	Hour	Summary of Events and Information	Remarks and references to Appendices
	MARCH			
ERIE CAMP (G11C 6.2)	19th		Brigade Transport Officer Corp GANNAWAY went on Anti-gas course. Inspection of Transport by Veterinary Officer, who pronounced the animals to be in excellent condition + everything satisfactory. Pte COLLINGWOOD went on a course to CAMIERS. Baths for the Company at WINNIPEG CAMP.	
	20		Preparing to go into the line. C.O. went up in the morning. 2/Lt CUFF + HANKS went up at 1.30 p.m. Rest of the Company paraded 5.35 p.m. + marched to LILLE GATE, YPRES. No 4 section proceeded to ZILLEBEKE Substation. No 3 to OBSERVATORY RIDGE, No 1 & RUDKIN HOUSE + No 2 to Reserve at BUND. Relief of 116th Coy. Complete 11.20 p.m.	
ZILLEBEKE BUND	21		Shelling of the tram line + duck boards + railway began in the morning; + became more intense later. At 3.25 p.m Shelling was concentrated on own end of the BUND line until 4.2 + 5.9 pm. Direct hits were Mess in, duck boards destroyed, dug-outs + Shelters A, B, C, D came through the map of Officers mess, pioneers hut walls + exposed Hay.	

Army Form C. 2118.

WAR DIARY
INTELLIGENCE SUMMARY.
(Erase heading not required.)

No. .... 62 ....

118TH MACHINE GUN

Place	Date 1917	Hour	Summary of Events and Information	Remarks and references to Appendices
ZILLEBEKE BUND.	MARCH			
	22		attack, stopping off a true. No casualties except one man of 117th team in Reserve wounded.	
OBSERVATORY RIDGE) SECTION			A quiet day and very little reported from our positions. A succession of short heavy snowstorms with sun and again a little sunshine throughout the day. Reserve section busily employed rebuilding latrines and officers mess, damaged the previous day.	
	23		A fine day with a cold N.E. wind. In the morning the Brigadier General visited the M.G. positions in the line with the C.O. Everything appeared satisfactory. There was the usual artillery activity throughout the day. 10 - 6 p.m. LILLE GATE and environs were very heavily shelled for half an hour. 2nd Lt. THOMAS and Sgt. Simonds went on an anti-aircraft course.	
	24		A fine day and very good visibility with considerable aerial activity. Also artillery activity. The enemy again shelled Cry Sign. Tho time around the orderly room. Fine 4.2 s falling in the vicinity	

Army Form C. 2118.

WAR DIARY
INTELLIGENCE SUMMARY.

(Erase heading not required.)

No......63........ 118TH MACHINE [GUN COY]

Place	Date 1917	Hour	Summary of Events and Information	Remarks and references to Appendices
ZILLEBEKE BUND OBSERVATORY RIDGE SUB-SECTION	MARCH			
		22365	2/Lt S.D. Roddick reported for duty from GRANTHAM also Lt N.R. CRUM-EWING who returned to ENGLAND 18.3.5.C. S.M. ROBERTS. W. reported for duty as C.S.M. (from No 12 M.G. Coy) in place of 21982 C.S.M. BOWYER. G. L/Cpl PETTIT reported back from aircraft course. Summer time came into force. Watches being put on one hour at	
	25	11. p.m.	Considerable enemy artillery activity throughout the day. The N.W. face of the BUND was again shelled until 4.25 in the evening one direct hit being obtained on the Officers Mess Cookhouse roof. Considerably damaging it & 2nd into Wrecking it in. RUDKIN H.S.F. was also heavily shelled for 20 mins at the same time damaging the tunnels in this place. There was a good deal of wind & flying one hostile machine presumably flying up and down our lines fired guns fired on it, over 2000 rounds. Lost from the BUND and one at STAFFORD ST. with good effect. Orders S/3 M.G.U/4.B.N. Lift no 16 to 20 K.R.R.E. 3rd Division. 2/Lt E. Johnson also t/f	

Army Form C. 2118.

118TH
No. 64

WAR DIARY
or
INTELLIGENCE SUMMARY.
(Erase heading not required.)

MACHINE GUN

Place	Date 1917	Hour	Summary of Events and Information	Remarks and references to Appendices
ZILLEBEKE BUND (OBSERVATORY RIDGE SECTION)	MARCH 26		For Transportation Depot Boulogne. At 12.25 A.M. the enemy raided our Brigade front with some force but was repulsed before reaching our lines by Lewis gun fire causing between 30 & 40 dead in front of our wire. The Brigadier congratulated the 4/5 Black Watch & 1/f Herts on their discipline. Our guns from RUDKIN H.S.G. fired 1250 rounds. A very quiet day with daylight rain and poor visibility. 2nd Lt HANKS was taken ill at RUDKIN HOUSE and was sent to hospital, but quickly recovered and returned to duty.	
	27		A quiet day with poor visibility until 5 p.m. when a change took place and caused considerable artillery and aerial activity. 116 M. G. Coy. relieved this company in the OBSERVATORY RIDGE Sector, which then moved across into the Left Brigade Sector relieving 117 M. G. Coy. No 2. Section under Lt RODDICK moved up from the BUND into the left Sub-sector and No 4 Section from ZILLEBEKE to the right Sub-sector. No 1 Section from RUDKIN H.S.E. to the BUND and No 3 from left tunnel Lees on Wear at ZILLEBEKE to Company Headquarters at LILLE GATE	

T2134. Wt. W708—776. 500000. 4/16. Sir J. C. & S.

Army Form C. 2118.

No. 65

WAR DIARY
INTELLIGENCE SUMMARY.
(Erase heading not required.)

Place	Date 1917	Hour	Summary of Events and Information	Remarks and references to Appendices
	MARCH			
	27(cont⁰)		The completion of relief was rather late 3.30 A.M (28ᵗʰ) owing to the new summer time and to the fact that the tunnels were packed with infantry when delayed movement. Good visibility but nothing of note happened except intermittent shelling of ZILLEBEKE BUND in vicinity of Section Hqrs, all through the morning and afternoon. A direct hit was obtained on the Dummy station near by. CAPT. CLOKEY returned to duty from Divisional Hqr. 2ᴺᴰ LT CUTTS went on a course of Lachiel Exercise under G.S.O X Corps at STEENVOORDE. Pte C.E. HUGHES reported to duty as Interpreter from Base.	
YPRES HOOGE SECTION	28		Very quiet day on the whole. The C.O and WELLERINGTON made an extended tour of the Sector.	
	29			
	30		A fairly lively day. Enemy shelling YPRES intermittently throughout the day also ZILLEBEKE BUND with 4.2" & 5.9". Our M.G's fired 1,500 rounds on to tramway and trenches in the vicinity of STIRLING CASTLE from HALF WAY HOUSE	

WAR DIARY

INTELLIGENCE SUMMARY

Army Form C. 2118.

118TH 66 MACHINE GUN COY.

Place	Date	Hour	Summary of Events and Information	Remarks and references to Appendices
	1917			
YPRES (HOOGE SECTION)	MARCH 31		2 Lieut THOMAS and 21986 Serjt SIMONDS returned from A.A. course	
			21992 L/Cpl WEBSTER Gwent on AA course	
			21982 Cpl PETTIT. Having been recommended for promotion to Serjt for duty at GRANTHAM proceeded to England	AG's letter 6864 1/23 10/16
			Very quiet day in back areas but a good deal of shelling in front line system. Reserve section were employed to-day on construction of elephant dugout $ at Coy H.Q.	
			Weather; fair some showers of sleet	

E.H. Fegher Capt
Comd.g 118th M.G. Coy

CONFIDENTIAL

War Diary

of

118th Machine Gun Company

From :- 1st April, 1917. — To :- 30th April, 1917.

(Volume II)

J.H.Cohen Capt.,
Commanding 118th Machine Gun Company.

Date :- 30th April, 1917.

Army Form C. 2118.

WAR DIARY
or
INTELLIGENCE SUMMARY.
(Erase heading not required.)

118TH MACHINE GUN [stamp]

Place	Date	Hour	Summary of Events and Information	Remarks and references to Appendices
YPRES	1/1/17	9.45-10.15am	Enemy Artillery active against WELLINGTON CRESCENT with 77MM shell. No damage done to trenches.	
		10.30-Noon	Enemy shelled ZILLEBEKE Rd at point I.22.6.86 where RE dump is, with 4.2 + 77MM shell. also DORMY House in Square I.22.a (mid) S.9" + 77 MM ae through the afternoon. Enemy appear to be registering on the left Batt. M.G. posh. I.e. in vecont of the CULVERT. Bn M.G's fired 1500 Rds during the night from HALFWAY Ho on Enemy trenches from I.18875-05/5 a 1" action of STIRLING CASTLE. J.13.c.05.70. when Enemy very very active. — Snowy day. Halfe Paled Very quiet day in the vicinity.	
"	2/1/7	3.30	" " active against WELLINGTON CRES. + RITZ ST. (near DORMY House) Using shells of all calibre up to 8". Southen End of WELLINGTON CRESCENT very damaged. Own M.G's fired from HALFWAY H.O. Co Position right. Sect + through day. Sect. Coy were relieved by the 117 M.G. Coy in the Left Bn Sector M.the 39 Divisional front. On relief Section marched independently to ERIE Camp — — arriving at 4AM. Only persone	
ERIE CAMP	3/1/7		indefinitely to ERIE Camp [illegible] arriving at 4AM. Only persone	
G.11.c.8.5				
Sheet 28 NW				

WAR DIARY or INTELLIGENCE SUMMARY

Army Form C. 2118.

Place	Date	Hour	Summary of Events and Information	Remarks and references to Appendices
ERIE CAMP Sheet 28 NW S.H.C.B.4.	3/9/17		Fell in Coy west at 11.30. A.M. for medical insp.	
"	4/9/17		The Coy slept the morning cleaning arms, ammunition etc & checking all sect. stores. Afternoon devoted to games. Orders received from Bde that we shall Probably move on the 5th to (by Sheet 27 B&F.) the HOUTKERQUE Area	
HOUTKERQUE Sheet 27 B&F	5		The Coy including transport moved by march route to HOUTKERQUE. Convoy ERIE Camp at 11.30 A.M. arriving HOUTKERQUE at 4.15p.m. & billet was made at 7p.m. for dinner. A field kitchen was loaned to us for this purpose, by arrangement with the C.O. & Brigade. Very fine day.	
"	6		The Coy paraded from 9am – 1pm. Training incl. close order drill, Lewis Gun, Physical and " Practice is loop & pulley. Poor saddlery, Sm. drill. Sent to the afternoon. Thursday. A conference of all Bde HQ whilst the C.O. attended. Forms notified on the march to HOUTKERQUE were discussed.	
"	7		The Coy paraded from 9am – 1pm. Programme — Box was sick for drill, included — 10 am — Box Repeaters Physical Training. 10 am Stoppages Mechanism. Feeling in Lewis of new Anti-Aircraft Sight for M.G. weather changeable	

WAR DIARY
or
INTELLIGENCE SUMMARY.
(Erase heading not required.)

Army Form C. 2118.
No. 69
DATE...........

Place	Date	Hour	Summary of Events and Information	Remarks and references to Appendices
Sheet 27 B & E				
HOUTKERQUE	8		(SUNDAY). Coy Paraded 9-9.30 for inspection. + 9.45-10.30 for Physical drill. Chaplain C of E service was held in the village @ 3pm.	
"	9		The Coy paraded from 9 - 10.30 a/m for close order drill + "exercises for activity drill (country) Sim in difficulty(rotation) + at 10.45 - 1pm for ROUTE march. Section were marched independently, at intervals, of 230 yds. Patches had been synchronised + clock hour halts were made. Section were sent ahead returning to Coy who recommenced march ¼ hr later See very valuable additions 40/hr.	The Report
"	9	5.30 pm	Lecture by Lt. Col. BIDDER, "Corp M.G.O., on Trench routine + gun use for weather	glorious. Sunday weather summery.
"	10		The Coy paraded from 9am - 11.45am, for close order drill. P.T. + a Battery	
"	"		Review by the Base Bombing Officer.	
"	"	1.30 pm	Battery Parade. The Coy was marched to HERZEELE for bath. from weather	
"	11		The Coy Paraded 9am - 1pm for Bombing. close order drill. into section squads completed + advanced gun drill.	
"	"	5.30 pm	Lecture in Prep + Air Photos by the Base Intelligence Officer.	

Army Form C. 2118.

No. .... 4 ....
DATE : ....
MACHINE GUN CO.

WAR DIARY
or
INTELLIGENCE SUMMARY.
(Erase heading not required.)

Instructions regarding War Diaries and Intelligence Summaries are contained in F. S. Regs., Part II. and the Staff Manual respectively. Title pages will be prepared in manuscript.

Place	Date	Hour	Summary of Events and Information	Remarks and references to Appendices
SHEET 27 B/4 HOUTKERQUE	12/4/17		Coy paraded from 9 AM - 11am for Bombing & Revolver practice. The instruction by the new draw bombing & revolver practice. weather changeable	
"	13.4.17		Coy paraded from 9 - 11am for Saluting & Arms Drill. Advances from Ordl. Physical training. Stoppages, notes Dect. Competition. Batmen in M.G. Cp in Afternoon. sew uniform for Smith.	
"	14.4.17	9 - 9.30am	Parade for Elmer Ada Greis	
		9.45-1pm	Tactical Exercise. The orders for the Exercise were given to the Section Officers covered immediately before the Whole Parade, so that they had to think the Plan Sudly. The idea was :- two sections & "Y" Coy were to them by a certain route to a point where a convoy was likely to pass. The remaining two Sections were to work the with the convoy. The disposition of the Guns. Were the two double Sections got in touch were took place. The escort on both sides didn't meet enough near 7 Crson. The Bde Commander has passed & went through the firm posts with the C.O. & observed the Scheme. No O's He pointed out one or two errors but on the whole was pleased with the	

T2134. Wt. W708—776. 500000. 4/15. Sir J. C. & S.

WAR DIARY / INTELLIGENCE SUMMARY

Army Form C. 2118.

Place	Date	Hour	Summary of Events and Information	Remarks and references to Appendices
HOUTKERQUE	14.4.17		10y Lt Schmidt hander Carnel out. Weather good.	
	15.4.17		Coy Paraded 9.A.M for inspection. 9.45AM Coy assembled & specially examined by M.O. for scabies. No cases were found.	
		10.15 AM	Parade for Divine Service. Same in afternoon. Weather changeable	
	16/4		Coy Paraded 9AM — 1pm. Saluting — Arms drill — Bell Filling. P.T. Physical drill advanced fire drill Lectures on Hygiene & Section Officers. Weather fair	
			One section moved by Motor Lorries to the LINE taking over from B Section 9th M.1.96G M.G.C. occupied positions at (by Map Tunnel Road 28.N.W.W.) SARATOGA CAMP (I 1 d) LA BRIQUE (C20d) RENINGHURST CAMP (H 6 b) and the 8th in reserve at REIGERSBURG CAMP.	
S CAMP (ARZADS)	17/4	9AM	Coy paraded at 9 A.M. (less one section) to overland links Reserve following HqrsS camp.	
REF. TRENCH MAP 28 N.W.4.		1.45p	Coy marched to S. camp by made route army of Ypres. Weather good.	
	18/4		Coy Paraded from 9 AM — 1 pm for inspection & R.E. for experience trench work same. Gun lessons & inspection of all gun equipment. Improvement of Billets. Afternoon Games. Weather fair	
	19/4		Coy paraded from 9AM — 11AM. for saluting & close order drill. Advanced gun drill. Physical training Baths 1 — 3pm. Weather good	
	20/4		Coy paraded from 9AM — 1pm for saluting & close order drill. Medical lecture — Coy for to Kemp Compass	

Army Form C. 2118
No. 4
DATE

WAR DIARY
or
INTELLIGENCE SUMMARY
(Erase heading not required.)

Instructions regarding War Diaries and Intelligence Summaries are contained in F.S. Regs., Part II. and the Staff Manual respectively. Title pages will be prepared in manuscript.

Place	Date	Hour	Summary of Events and Information	Remarks and references to Appendices
(Kinmel May 28 Nov & A22 & 83) S. CAMP	20/5		Compy Hdqrs Inventory of Stretcher kits &c. Coys Drill Stoppages in the Range. Afternoon Tab in Coy boxes bandages for trenches.	
"		5p-5.30p	Lecture M.Gs - Open barrage. Lecture Cont. Nut & Spring Catch modified	day
	21/4	9-1p	Coy Parades for Inspection of Arms & Sy Equipment. Laws. Indication & Recognition of Target. Commrs will command Sectional Physical Drill. Tabs in boxes baby annual provision	
			Judging distance class 1 BTS Army tunic	
		2p	NCO's parade under 3 Lieut. Hanks (Physical Culture Expert) for Instruction in Physical Training. trench feet.	
"	22	9-9.30p	Coy Parade for Inspection by Sect Offrs.	
		10.15 "	Church Parade (in Camp) trench feet	
	23.	9-1p	Coy Parades for Saluting & Arms Drill. Demonstration of duties of Various Numbers. Physical Drill. Stoppages in McKay (Modern) Remain in advance gun drill Use of Cover. Morning Punch in Action. trench feet.	
	24.	9-1p	Coy Parade for Inspection of all Arms & Sig appliances within. Cavalry Rect inwards for trenches. Indiv Section Compy in Shipage bahn in M.G. action.	
		2-3p	Improvement of Kemps	

T2134. Wt. W708-776. 500000. 4/16. Sir J. C. & S.

Army Form C. 2118.

No. ....
DATE ....

WAR DIARY
or
INTELLIGENCE SUMMARY.
(Erase heading not required.)

Instructions regarding War Diaries and Intelligence Summaries are contained in F. S. Regs, Part II. and the Staff Manual respectively. Title pages will be prepared in manuscript.

Place	Date	Hour	Summary of Events and Information	Remarks and references to Appendices
S.Camp	24/4	5-5.30p	Section : Route for Recce/Recon. Weather fine.	
	25/4	9-1p	Parade for. Semaphore Signalling. Instruction in the Contract Drill & Test Screwing. Making	
			Range Card & Elbow Hitches. Colonel came for Stal	
		2.15-3.30p	Instruction in Map Reading.	
		5p-5.30p	Echo. Stationed both methods of Indirect fire.	
	26/4	9-1p	Parade for: ANK Say Drill. Tests in getting quickly into action. Contact with one officer & Physical Training. Stung Work on Section. General Practical Map & Compass work.	
			For the little work. Teams were given a tray of the District. (They were given as a few minutes to read it in and to say if we were given by the N.C.O. of the Team). A map reference was given & instructions to mount the gun on that spot, to fire in a certain direction. They were rested the places, how to site the gun, & by what map compass and it in the	
			rifle direction. [2LT O.MOODIE & 2.i.K Reinforcement by which platoon]	
		2p-3p	Inspection of K. Range.	
		3p-5.30p	Instruction - fitting lens in belts, receiver front	
Coy H.Q	27/4	9-9.30	Inspected of all arms for appearance & still with same.	
CANAL BK		9.30-1p	Preparation for going in to line	
Sheet 28 NW				
A 28 c 5.4				

WAR DIARY or INTELLIGENCE SUMMARY

Army Form C. 2118

Place	Date	Hour	Summary of Events and Information	Remarks and references to Appendices
CANAL BK 27.4 A28c54 Trench Map 28NW4	27.4		The Coy less one sectn moved off 4pm "S"CAMP at 7pm to relieve the 116 M.G.Coy in the HILLTOP Section. Ref. Map (Trench) Sheet 28 N.W.4. The Section at REIGERSBURG CHAT. The Section at CANAL BANK. H.Q. took over the positions of 116 Coy in the line. The Coy at CANAL BANK H.Q. took over the positions of 116 Coy in the line. Took No 9 gun in the trench 15. with 1 in reserve ("A" Coy H.Q.) (work it out) Relief Completed 12.30 AM 27/28	Ref MAP 1/10,000 ST JULIEN
"	28		Enemy G.Killer very quiet. Enemy M.G fired on an aeroplanes from neighbourhood of MORTELDJE sap. Six Enemy Planes come to our lines during the morning, they were fired on by the 1m plane & rifles. We used Vm Orne. Weather good	
"	29.	11 AM	Enemy Artillery active against HILLTOP. H.E shrapnel & 77 MM shell were used.	
		3 pm	Enemy again active against HILLTOP, using 77 M.M shells	
		4.30 p	One enemy aeroplane driven down by our airmen over POTIJZE	
		9.30 p	A dummy raid was carried out in the enemy front line between KEUPP Fm & CAESARS NOSE on M.Guns took part in this. Weather good.	
	30	12.30 AM	The 11th Bde in our right carried out a raid in the Subury trenches, 34 prisoners & a M.G	

Army Form C. 2118.

WAR DIARY
or
INTELLIGENCE SUMMARY.
(Erase heading not required.)

118TH
No. 1/5

Place	Date	Hour	Summary of Events and Information	Remarks and references to Appendices
CANAL BK.	30/4	12:30 am	Have captured. Our artillery & the Corps M.G. maintained a heavy barrage on the enemy's line whilst this was being carried out. Our M.G. fire at 12,000 Rds. The enemies counter barrage was very slight. Prisoners were all of the 392 I.R. The O.R. of the Coy slightly wounded. Enemy artillery very quiet during the day. Our M.G. fired over 5000 rounds on the enemies trenches + communication during the night. Weather good.	REF MAP Trench Sheet 28 NW 4 1/10000 ST JULIEN

J.H. Baker Capt
Comdg 118 MGCoy

Vol 13

CONFIDENTIAL.

War Diary

of

118th Machine Gun Company.

From :- 1st May, 1917 ~ To :- 31st May, 1917.

(Volume - II)

1/6/17.

Army Form C. 2118.

WAR DIARY
or
INTELLIGENCE SUMMARY.
(Erase heading not required.)

Instructions regarding War Diaries and Intelligence Summaries are contained in F. S. Regs., Part II. and the Staff Manual respectively. Title pages will be prepared in manuscript.

Place	Date	Hour	Summary of Events and Information	Remarks and references to Appendices
COY H.Q. CANAL BANK	1·5·17		Enemy artillery very quiet all day.	MAP REF: ST. JULIEN C.25 a.B.2
HILLTOP SECTOR		1AM-1.50AM.	Our M.Gs fired 5900 rounds on the Enemies trenches & communications during a raid carried out by the 11th Bde on our left.	See Appendix "A"
		12.30p.	Four Enemy aeroplanes were engaged by our aeroplanes between CANAL Bk H.Q. & VLAMERTINGHE. Only one Enemy Plane was seen to return. 100 rounds were fired at this Plane by the gun at LA BRIQUE.	
		8pm.	Another night took Place over YPRES, but the Enemy Planes succeeded in escaping.	
			Our M.Gs. fired during the night on area around Below Fm. MACKENSON Fm + gap in GERMAN wire in front of MORTELDJE. Rounds fired Total 3250.	
"	2·5·17		Enemy artillery quiet during the day. Fine day	
		12.30p.	Four Enemy aeroplanes were engaged behind our lines by our Planes. Only one Enemy Plane was seen to return	
		8pm	Another air fight took Place over YPRES, but the Enemy succeeded in escaping.	
			Our M.Gs fired during the night on area around Below Fm. MACKENSON Fm + gap in German wire in front of MORTELDJE. Rounds fired 3,250. Fine weather	
	3·5·17		Enemy artillery very quiet all day in our area. During the afternoon our Howitzers firing were in the direction of POPERINGHE	
		7pm	German Aeroplane Rattled our lines & WIEITJE. 90 rounds were fired at them from WILLOW Fm. gun	

WAR DIARY or INTELLIGENCE SUMMARY

Army Form C. 2118.

Place	Date	Hour	Summary of Events and Information	Remarks and references to Appendices
Coy H.Q. CANAL BK. HILLTOP SECTOR	3.5.17		Gun position	MAP REF ST JULIEN
		10.10 p.m	Geo reported from our left flank. All small arms Respirators were put on & Stretchers been sounded	
		10.40 p.m	All clear reported. Our M.G.s fired during the night on draw-ways around CIVILIZATION FM. & on GAP at C16.C.27 3,500 rounds fired. Weather fine.	
	4.5.17	4.15 a.m	Enemy put about 18 4.2" shells near our Gun position at CLIFFORD TOWERS (C21.a.38)	
		9.30 a.m	About six Enemy Planes passed over our lines, returning to their own lines about 9.45 a.m.	
		4 p.m	About 10 enemy planes flew over our lines, but with no apparent result. Our M.G. at C16.c.15" fired 1000 lbs during the night on MOUSE TRAP FM (C.26.c.77.). Weather good.	
	5.5.17		Enemy shelled the chalk bank leading from LA.B.RIGUE to CANAL BK. during the morning & again in the afternoon.	
		11.30 a.m	The Heavies flung Nit ad fing (CLIFFORD) TOWERS (about C.21.a.38) were shelled by the Enemy. The M.G store next to our house blown in. Some of the men Kit & Equipment was destroyed.	
		7.30 p.m	Our M.G. at MACGREGORS lost ( ) fired 100 lbs on Boche planes which were flying at low altitude	

WAR DIARY
or
INTELLIGENCE SUMMARY.

Army Form C. 2118.

118TH

Place	Date	Hour	Summary of Events and Information	Remarks and references to Appendices
Coy HQ CANAL BK	25.5.17		Attitude over own front line	Ref map ST JULIEN
		6AM.	Own M.G.s fired 400 rounds during the night on Enemy knobs + transport. Scout weather
		6AM	(CLIFFORD) TOWERS again to be shelled by McInery
			Enemy artillery was more active during the day
		9.30AM.	Several "SIG" pits on HILL TOP
		2.30PM	Heavy Shrapnel over HILL TOP. Area shelled enough Fm will S.9
			ST JEAN. Was shelled considerably during the day.
		6p	Three enemy planes reported have been brought down in our lines
		8p.	250 rounds fired by our M.G. at WILSON Fm. Enemy plane flying low over our lines
			Bw M.G. fired during the night on CANADIAN RESERVE CIVILIZATION Fm. tavern front of
			GALANDER TRENCH M. 6.500 rounds fired. Aeroplane fired
			Enemy Artillery fairly quiet during the day
"	7.5.17	1.15p.	8 Clay photograph his ordered especially behind KEMMEL HILL
		7.45p	About 12 HE shells burst in vicinity of LONE WILLOWS.
		7.55p	5 Lt. H.2" were dropped in vicinity of LA BELLE ALLIANCE. Three of them appeared to be "BLIND". He first one has burst on a meridian still as is with the figure in his ledge in the when I fell

WAR DIARY or INTELLIGENCE SUMMARY

Army Form C. 2118.

Place	Date	Hour	Summary of Events and Information	Remarks and references to Appendices
Coy H.Q. CANAL BK	7/5/17			REF. MAP ST JULIEN
	8/5/17		Own M.G.s fired during the night to harass Road & tramway from C15d6575 – c2d8505, CANADIAN Reserve & the road CIVILIZATION FM. 4000 Rds fired. Weather fine. Enemy Artillery firing fairly all day.	
"		3.30pm	What appeared to be two ammunition dumps were blown up in enemy lines in direction of MARSOUIN FM.	
		8pm	Five 4.5 billetine shrapnel vicinity of IRISH & ENGLISH FM.	
		8.45pm	Several eight shells (77mm) thrown between julia vicinity of CLIFFORD Towers. Own MGs fired during the night on area round CIVILIZATION FM. Tramways & junction with CALENDER AV & CANADIAN Reserve. 4000 Rounds fired. Twenty shots fired W.G.N Cuffe granted 18 days special leave to U.K. from the 9th. Enemy Artillery active against CLIFFORD Towers.	
	9/5/17	10 am	It has been reported that own M.G. fire on MORTELDJE S.P. was successful in keeping down enemy snipers. Own MGs fired 5250 Rounds during the night in Roads & tramways from C27c8510 & Road tramways & trench around YANITEULE FM. & C17d2080. On CANADIAN Reserve. Weather fine.	
	10/5/17		Enemy Artillery quiet throughout the day. Enemy Aeroplane came over our lines at	

T2134. Wt. W708–776. 500000. 4/15. Sir J. C. & S.

Army Form C. 2118.

WAR DIARY
or
INTELLIGENCE SUMMARY.
(Erase heading not required.)

Place	Date	Hour	Summary of Events and Information	Remarks and references to Appendices
CANAL BK.	10/5/17		About again at 9pm. The M.Gs fired in bk. Jetty B 1100 Rds. The enemy at	Ref MAP ST JULIEN
		9pm.	closed Hey sudden 4 made off for their lines.	
			The M.Gs fired during the night on lines between Point C15d42.78 - C15d85.53 +	
			between C15a 60.80 - C15d 20.90 also attacks from C18d 25.35 - C17e 50.70. Rounds fired 5.500	
	11/5/17	7:30PM.	Enemy dropped C. 77.MM shells about C21a 20.80. Showing his artillery was quiet -	
			Snipers were active Rifle shot firing from MORTELDJE GAP towards CLIFFORD TOWERS	
		9-9.15p.m	Our M.Gs in BURNT FM fired on C15d 6 8. by arrangements made with OS Battalion Lef	
			attacks. 750 Rds fired. 500 Rds were fired during the night on area around	
			CIVILIZATION FM.	
	12/5/17	8:20p.	Enemy Put 3.77MM shells into trench near VIEW FM	
		11.AM	6. Heavy Shrapnel shells were Put on HILL TOP by the enemy.	
		8.15p.	Enemy put about 10. 5.9 + 4.2" Shells about C20d 40.35. One .4.5" dropped in	
			Mens Latrine - I about 16 more near LA BELLE ALLIANGE	
			Our M.G fired during the night on pillars from BURNT FM. on CALENDER FE's	
			+ CANADIAN RESERVE from C15b 55.25 - C15b 90.08 - from WILSON FM. on	
			Enemy front line between C.22a 95.45 - C22b 15.30 + on junction of trench

Army Form C. 2118.

WAR DIARY
or
INTELLIGENCE SUMMARY.
(Erase heading not required.)

Instructions regarding War Diaries and Intelligence Summaries are contained in F.S. Regs., Part II. and the Staff Manual respectively. Title pages will be prepared in manuscript.

No. 81

Place	Date	Hour	Summary of Events and Information	Remarks and references to Appendices
CANAL BK	Conta 12/5/17 (13/5/17)		Shown map D C23695.90. Rounds fired 2,500. Weather fine but hazy. Enemy artillery very quiet all day. Nine enemy planes were observed over our lines during the evening. Our AA. MGs fired 1250 Rds at them. Our MGs fired during the night on MOUSE TRAP FM., to C.16 & 12 crossroads from C9d 83.30 — C9d 95.12. On streets from C.15 & 3 81 — C.15 E 15.90. 4000 Rds fired. Weather fine.	REF MAP ST. JULIEN
	14/5		Enemy artillery quiet all day. From BURNT FM — 8:30 AM. An Enemy aeroplane was observed to be led to forced to descend just behind our lines. 9/13/pts	
		3 PM	An Enemy Plane passed over Coy HQ flying very low in southerly direction. It was hit, shelled by our AA arta."	
			Our MGs fired during the night on gaps in CALIBAN TR. firing 10,000 Rds between midnight & dawn.	
		11:45p	Our MGs fired on CANADIAN RESERVE, CALF RESERVE to Enemy's communications during a raid carried out by 1/1 Cambs Rgt. Our MG opened with the artillery fire at 12:25 am (14/15). 15,500 Rounds were fired.	
	15	10am	Enemy put over about 20. S.G" & 4.7" Shells in vicinity Fort F— & ZOUAVE VILLA. Enemy artillery quiet during remainder of the day. Weather fine. The raid by the 1/1 CAMBS Rgt was successful. 2 Prisoners were taken.	

WAR DIARY
INTELLIGENCE SUMMARY

Army Form C. 2118.

No. ....
DATE ....

Place	Date	Hour	Summary of Events and Information	Remarks and references to Appendices
CANAL BK.	16/5		Enemy artillery normal. Quiet day	REF MAP. ST JULIEN.
		10.30a.	The 116 MC Coy arrived & relies the Coy in the line. On completing relief our section 1 gun to take over from the section of the 116 Coy in RUGERSBURG Posture.	
'S' CAMP. A.22.d.6.3	17.	6.30AM.	Relief complete: all teams from Nos 4 & 5 in the RUGERS BURG Posture arrive in 'S' Camp. No work done till 6.30pm when gun teams were overhauled & gun Kits checked.	REF. MAP SHEET 28 NW EDIT. 5a
"	18.		Coy paraded 9.AM for close order drill & gas drill. Remainder of day spent in cleaning up. Weather good	
"	19.		Coy paraded from 9 AM - 1pm to Inspection of drill and smoke box Apparatus; Semaphore, Physical drill, Mechanism of Gun & Lamp. Elementary gun drill & from 5p - 5.30p to instruction in marking of map & range.	
"	20		Coy paraded for inspection & drum service. 2Lt Cuth reported back from leave. Lt CRAWLEY reported back from M.G. Course. CAMIERS.	
"	20			
"	21		Coy paraded from 9 A.M - 12.30.p. for Cabling & close order drill; Semaphore, gun drill, Physical drill. Instruction in laying from map & compass. Instruction in leaving PACK & carrying Helio from PACK animal. 2Lt. DAVIES reported for duty from BASE Depot.	

Army Form C. 2118.
No. 83

WAR DIARY
INTELLIGENCE SUMMARY
(Erase heading not required.)

Instructions regarding War Diaries and Intelligence Summaries are contained in F.S. Regs., Part II. and the Staff Manual respectively. Title pages will be prepared in manuscript.

Place	Date	Hour	Summary of Events and Information	Remarks and references to Appendices
S CAMP A 22.d.6.3.	22/5		Coy paraded from 8.30AM to 12.30p- for Respirator & Hyperaeris/ instructn & Marching. 1.30 p-word received in Map & Compass. Marching given a given direction by Map & Compass. We relieved the Section of PETERSBURG COPSE during the night. Orders received from Bde head qrs no section to relieve 1 team of 164 Coy MGC in WIELTJE Sub section, the men duly carried out the Coy'ers no anti tk/ gas sections at S. Camp. weather good	Rgt. Branch Map Sheet 28 NW EDT 5a
	23/5	8.30AM — 12.30p-	Coy paraded from 8.30AM to 12.30p- for Section drills, including Clare Over view, Semaphore, Ceremonial gun drill, including Stoppages, Hyperaerial, the 9 General Rules. weather good	
		from 2.30 — 4p-	Same	
	24/5	8.30AM — 12.30p-	Coy paraded at 8.30Am for Route march, including Reconnaissance by Officers + men,	
		2.30p- — 3.30p-	to Indoor Truct Recognitn of targets using fine weather good	
		5 p- — 5.30p-	Lecture on Tanks from head Reconnaissance Reports.	
	25/5	8.30 — 12.30p-	Parade from 8.30 - 12.30p- for Semaphore, Clune over Drill, practice in Lifts & Bumps Tins, Hyperaerial Drill, Lewis Gun-Stuck-Actn Reps. etc.	
		2.30p- 4p-	Instructn to Pack Teamwork Drilling. tcp. Maxim. weather good	

Army Form C. 2118.

WAR DIARY
or
INTELLIGENCE SUMMARY.
(Erase heading not required.)

Instructions regarding War Diaries and Intelligence Summaries are contained in F.S. Regs., Part II. and the Staff Manual respectively. Title pages will be prepared in manuscript.

Place	Date	Hour	Summary of Events and Information	Remarks and references to Appendices
S CAMP AZZd 6.3	MAY 26		Conference from 8.30am - 12.30pm. Answers Drill. Semaphone. Quick Loading? Gun in defence. Map reading; physical drill, instruction in fight for passage of gun. Section at WIEITJE instructed, relieved by section of 116 Coy M.G.C. also the PILCKEM section by the 118 Coy. Weather good.	Ref MAP Sheet Ypres 28 N.W. ED 50.
	27		Reg. Parade 8.4 p.m. for baths; all sections had dim change of under clothing. No new instruction. Weather good. (Sunday)	
	28		Conferenced for saluting, telephone drill, advance of Bull advances for instruction in Blue and Eye. Physical turning, Gas and Oxygen memory. Brigade instruction in quick mounts after ½ top shower mg. Practice Range dark. Sent up to Hill 60 top sector. (Engels Farm) Knuth arrangement for Machine Gun Post traverse night. They are K hour. buffets at this Pointe selected, & then moved in Reserve. Bomb shots for the night. Weather good. The M.G. shoot in co-operation with the guns of 116 & 117 Coys. approached	

Army Form C. 2118.

No. 85

WAR DIARY
or
INTELLIGENCE SUMMARY.
(Erase heading not required.)

118TH

Place	Date	Hour	Summary of Events and Information	Remarks and references to Appendices
S. Camp A 2 d. 63	May 28		Artillery 7.38' to 5.55 Bn also on our Bn's M.G. north in Support Sngl. Capt. E.H. Clarke C.O. the M.G. groups on our front. Lt. R. Filkins 1st — in charge of M.G. Coy Group. One is directed against Enemy trenches in Squares C23. a & c. due h. & commence with rafale, ceasing 130 yds. every 4 minutes. Rate w/fire 6 guns 500 yds. south to home.	By MAP (Trend) Sheet 28 NW ED.50 By MAP ST JULIEN
"	29		Coy Parades from 6:30am—9am for Semaphore, Inspection, Vacant for experience & drill with Sword, Bayonet etc from 2nd army Contained Sight, Hyposite Sight, Range Cards etc. Also Lectures 2:30p—4:15p. Instruction — Lift to Barricade. Machine Gun Shot Protection 2 hours — weather good but hazy.	
"	30		Parades from 8:30am—12:30p for Saluting & Close order drill, Gun drill, wearing the Respirator, Physical Drill, Marching to a selected spot by map & mounting guns in given direction by Map & Compass. Games in afternoon. The MG shoot was carried out by No 2 Section which had remained the night at Rencksburg Cross. Both sections were in their position at	

WAR DIARY
INTELLIGENCE SUMMARY

Army Form C. 2118.

Place	Date	Hour	Summary of Events and Information	Remarks and references to Appendices
'S' CAMP A.28.c.6.3	MAY 30		6.27 to 18.65 (approx) ready to open fire at 5.30 p.m. The shoot commenced at 6 p.m. & lasted 14 mins. First elevations were all put on by Clinometer, & the remaining elevations did not leave remain by elevations received from by the dial. Fire was controlled by the Officer in charge of each battery, & from the Group having been split into two batteries. Lieut. CRAWLEY in charge of right batty, & 2/LT ROOKE in charge of left Batty. The right batty, commenced fire at 5.59 p.m. According to arrangement, it preceded the left Batty by two minutes at that successive lift, so that there was always one Batty in action, also the guns were so laid that each hit East batty covered with own fire the front allotted to the group. Both batteries ceased fire at 6.14 p.m. Total No of rounds fired by the group was 11.000. Much annual defect noted these. One gun had two broken firing pins, & two holes in the top of barrel casing of another gun lit in steam. The two No 5 plugged will continue trials of fire decreased. A third gun had a prolonged stoppage through one of the holts of front cover cold, breaking & jamming between the	Ry MAP Sheet 28 NW & ST JULIEN

WAR DIARY or INTELLIGENCE SUMMARY

Army Form C. 2118.

Place	Date	Hour	Summary of Events and Information	Remarks and references to Appendices
S CAMP Area 6.3.	MAY 30		Between the barrel leech + sleeve concealment can food + ammunition crawled out into shell holes with the guns etc + returned CAMP 4. from where they returned to S. CAMP.	Ref MAP Sheet 28 NW + ST JULIEN
"	31		All teams after firing were manned by Reichsburg after dark. Route reconnaissance Parade at 8.30 am. for Route MARCH, including Route reconnaissance by Officers. 2.30-3.35p. Indication + Recognition targets various game. 5p-5.45p. Points from Route Reconnaissance reports. Weather fine.	
		9+5 pm	One 9 am Aircraft followers near the Camp brought down by Boche aeroplane. the Enemy plane made good its escape.	

J H Colver Capt
Comdg 118 M.G. Coy.

Ref MAP.
ST. JULIEN

Appendix A

Reference. our MG fire on night of 30/1st May in support of raid carried out by 114th Inf Bde. Zero hour was 1.AM. 1st MAY. Fire to be maintained for 50 mins. Following is list of Gun Positions used. Target. + Rate of fire

No of Guns.	Position of Gun.	Target	Rate of Fire
1	C20c05.55. (BURNT. FM)	CAKE LANE from Front line to KOHN FM.	20 rounds at ½ min intervals
1	C21b.15.10 (HILL TOP)	CALEDONIA Reserve from C15a40.50 up to HINDENBURG FM.	do
1	C20b95.45 (LA BELLE ALLIANCE)	CALEDONIA TRENCH + CALEDONIA SUPPORT. EAST of C15a.20.15.	do

Total Rounds fired 5.900

Vol 14

CONFIDENTIAL

War Diary

of

118th Machine Gun Company.

From - 1st June, 1917. to - 30th June, 1917

(Volume II)

WAR DIARY

Army Form C. 2118.

118th
M.G.C. — GUN CO.

Place	Date	Hour	Summary of Events and Information	Remarks and references to Appendices
S. CAMP A.22.d.8.3	June 1917 1	8:30 AM –12:30 p	Coy paraded from 8:30 AM – 12:30 pm. for saluting & close order drill. Shrapnel including M.G. Signal, Gun Drill. Physical Drill. Instruction in laying gun by map & Compass.	Ref MAP TRENCH Sheet 28NW Ed. 5.
		2:30pm – 4pm	Instruction in lifts for Barrage fire.	ST JULIEN 28NW5
		8:30pm	4 two sections sent guns etc moved into the line Hill 70 T Sector. For more preparation for a practice M.G. Barrage Tomorrow morning.	
	2		1st Section at Coy H.Q. S. Camp paraded from 8:30am – 12:30pm. for Semaphore, reading MG Signal. Inspection & adjust for apparent and actual zone. Advanced drill using combined sights, Physical Drill. Marching firing in different positions.	
		2:30 – 4pm	Games.	
		4:30pm	The two sections in the line commanded practice barrage in conjunction with Artillery. Location of this Coop Group V Target 9pm = C27.b.18.68. 2ndary was checked German trench in C 23 a +c. to valley fire serial + 1. Lifts etc. See APPENDIX I. The group ceased fire at 4:40pm. Inspect men left in position in antrepots. 2 Another practice shoot tomorrow. Guns communication ran left at LA BRIQUE and a cleaning party & guard. Remainder of the Section were taken back to Reigersburg CAMP for the night weather good.	See APPENDIX I.

Army Form C. 2118.

WAR DIARY
or
INTELLIGENCE SUMMARY.
(Erase heading not required.)

Instructions regarding War Diaries and Intelligence Summaries are contained in F. S. Regs., Part II. and the Staff Manual respectively. Title pages will be prepared in manuscript.

Place	Date	Hour	Summary of Events and Information	Remarks and references to Appendices
S CAMP A.22.d.8.3	June 3		HKs section at Coy HQ. Paraded two for inspection & drew service rifles. The HKs section in the line having relieved ones for another practice for to-day.	R/MAP Trench Sheet 58NW EDT 5 + ST JULIEN 28 NW 2
		3 p.m.	Open traced this position ST C 27.6.18.6.8. Firing commenced at Zero +15 to 3.15 p.m. Continued in 15 min. The Shelter fired from Zero to +30 for Raised, elevations etc. See APPENDIX 2. Enemy retaliation was very feeble & all yesterday practice. No but several S.9" on BURNT P.M. but nothing fell near our group positions whole day.	See APPENDIX 2
	4		On completion of shoot all sections Cameron will gun supports to be Rendezvous CRATE & then after dark to S. CAMP. Weather good. Two sections paraded from 8:30 – 12:30 for instruction in Saluting, Close Order drill, Semaphore morning M.G. Stunt. Advance of gun, Repair of Gun, Use of Ground Cover, 2:30 – 4 p.m. Gunch & Cameron & Instruction organizing range W.O.112. The Remains of kit declared damaged from etc & returned then for equipment after the shoots of the 2nd & 3rd June. A Lance Corporal & an Ok. Aircraft Battery reported for duty until 13/June for purpose	

Army Form C. 2118.

WAR DIARY
or
INTELLIGENCE SUMMARY.
(Erase heading not required.)

Instructions regarding War Diaries and Intelligence Summaries are contained in F.S. Regs., Part II. and the Staff Manual respectively. Title pages will be prepared in manuscript.

Place	Date	Hour	Summary of Events and Information	Remarks and references to Appendices
S.CAMP a22a 8.3	June 4 Cont'd		Of instruction. Officers & O.R.'s in recognition of our own & Enemy aeroplanes. Weather good. RE.	Ref Map Sheet 28 NW Sect "S"
	5		H/Coy runs two teams. Parade 9am. 8:30am - 12:30pm for instruction in MG Signals & Atmosphere, Gun Drill including 15 mins with box respirators on, Physical Drill, Marching to a detailed spot by Map & Compass & mounting gun at given direction by MAP & Compass. 2:30pm – 4:15pm. Practice in lifts for Barrage fire. The ^ received instruction in Recognition of our own Enemy aircraft. Weather good. RE.	
S.CAMP a22a 8.3	6		The Coy Minor Sections 8:30 – 12:30 & 2:30 – 4:15 for instruction in Saddling & Close Order Drill. Inspector Visitants for appearance. Joined Service Reconnu. his section made Lt Brawley & 2Lt Gults cleaned Guns & driven Mooring & moved into new H.L.T.R.P. Sector. Occupied Light Gun Posten at C23d 18.68 ready to take part in coming operations at a time to be notified later. Weather good. RE.	
	7	3AM	Our Light Guns at C23b 18.68 opened fire on enemy trenches in C23 a.t.c. according to Barrage Time Table (see Appendix 3) 6 minutes in offensive	See Appendix 3

WAR DIARY or INTELLIGENCE SUMMARY.

Army Form C. 2118.

Place	Date	Hour	Summary of Events and Information	Remarks and references to Appendices
S. CAMP. a 22 a 8.3	7.	anti 3.30	Operations taking place just S. 1/2 - of MESSINES. The guns were ranged in batteries of 4. Simpson a. on 2nd & 3rd June. The batteries while firing were only slightly troubled by enemy shelling. The N.C.O.s being slightly wounded. Both batteries fired for 20 minutes all guns getting off their allotted nº of belts. to Coming out of the line Sergt Bryan the man in Sergt. Shea's gun team was killed & his teamer by a hit. which fell to his hand. Both Sections moved to RUDERSBURG CHATEAU where they had breakfast, after which the Section him Sergt. moved to the S. Camp. Sergt. Supers. Sections were moved from RUDERSBURG CHAT. after dark by limber to S. Camp. Remainder of Coy passed from 8.30 - 12.30pm for motivation Gunsights, from Drill, Rapid fire Drill, mechanism & Stoppages 2.30pm - 4.15pm Instruction in Sights Occupation of sights & top traverse etc. Lectures Gun 1.15	
WORMHOUDT Ref map.	8.		The Coy moved by train to WORMHOUDT. Leaving POPERINGHE Stat 9.35 arriving WORMHOUDT 12.45pm. Transport moved by road arriving 2.30pm	
HAZEBROUCK 5 a	9.		Coy paraded 9AM. - 12.30pm for general clean up. 2h — 4.15 hr Recreational training. The two forms of elimination contest for Bisques sports recruits took 125	

Army Form C. 2118.

WAR DIARY
or
INTELLIGENCE SUMMARY.
(Erase heading not required.)

Instructions regarding War Diaries and Intelligence Summaries are contained in F.S. Regs., Part II. and the Staff Manual respectively. Title pages will be prepared in manuscript.

Place	Date	Hour	Summary of Events and Information	Remarks and references to Appendices
WORMHOUDT	10		Coy paraded for Divine Service + Bath. Weather fine	Ref MAP. HAZEBROUK 5A
OCHTEZEELE	11		The Coy moved to new Billets at OCHTEZEELE passing through	HAZEBROUK 5A
			Junction of ESQUEBECK + LEDRINGHEM Rd at C10.d.1. (Ref MAP Sheet 27 Belgium & France)	do
		11.30 AM	arriving OCHTEZEELE 5pm. Route followed as through LEDRINGHEM + ARNEKE. Weather good. RS.	
ESQUERDES	12		The Coy moved to his Billets S. ESQUERDES en route to training Area	Ref MAP SH 5E 27
			passing Starting Point at N16.a.u.7 @ 7.39 AM arriving ESQUERDES	Belgium + FRANCE +
		5.30pm	Weather good. 11.OR's fell out but were brought	HAZEBROUK 5A
			along @ Pace 7 Power by a 3 Tonner. Route:- CLAIR MARAIS.	
			ARQUES. WIZERNES. HALLINES.	
WATTERDAL	13		The Coy moved to his Billets at WATTERDAL (in vicinity of having promot)	
			Marching in rear of 4/5 Black Watch. from starting Point, Railway Crossing	
			LUMBRES @ 10.55 am arriving WATTERDAL 1.30pm. No oN.fell out.	
			Weather good. RS.	
	14		Coy paraded 9AM for General Clean up.	
			All officers with exception of Orderly Officer reconnoitred Training Ground.	

Army Form C. 2118.

WAR DIARY
or
INTELLIGENCE SUMMARY.
(Erase heading not required.)

Instructions regarding War Diaries and Intelligence Summaries are contained in F.S. Regs., Part II. and the Staff Manual respectively. Title pages will be prepared in manuscript.

Place	Date	Hour	Summary of Events and Information	Remarks and references to Appendices
WATERDAL			Training going on in Area enclosed by boundaries HUMBRES. HARLETTES. WESTBECOURT. VAL d'ACQUIN. LE PLOURE	REF MAP HAZEBROUCK 5A
	15		Coy paraded from 8:30 - 12:30 & 2:30 - 4p.m. Physical drill, Anticipation, Packing limbers & Pack Gun wrk, Mechanism, Semaphore, rectifying stoppages, clean guns, open/safety. Lednie. Experiencing readings & following days work recorder. Sgt. K.R.	
	16		Coy. moved off at 8:30 am for tram ground at Carpopt. with 16 fighting Programme. Practice with Pack Saddles. Range firing Irrecurlin & kneeling. semaphore are many carried out — — — — fully taken. Gun reports were taken to Gilkury in cost. Arms as Needle good.	
	17		Coy paraded for inspection & drive service, an advance exposition made following days work. Weather got 25.	
	18		The Coy moved the dect- manouvred at 8:30 a.m. to tram ground at carried out the following programme. Practices & manyl Carryin firm — to Cutwork. Range firing. Range card. Remaing sectn. were attending to hear & the 1/I CAMBS Rep. tutr. Part in a battalion scheme	

WAR DIARY / INTELLIGENCE SUMMARY

Army Form C. 2118.

Place	Date	Hour	Summary of Events and Information	Remarks and references to Appendices
	Cont II			REF-MAP?
WATEROAL	18		March K. having joined Coln Kn horses. The morning having been at the handustan in afternoon. RS.	HAZEBROUCK 5A
"	19		The Coy took part in a Brigade Scheme in the morning. Scheme consisted in column of route with transport to move SE OMAR - BOULOGNE (Bd head) Column in close order movements SW of A.L. HARLETTES at 9AM. 1/2 Sect. allotted to 1/c CHESHIRE Regt. 1 sect — to 4/5 BLACK WATCH. 2/c Section in support Immediately o/c commenced of operat— 10.45 AM. the section (+ supports) was put in at 7 6cts of the trenches.It having come under enemy M.G. fire. The O/C Coy forth with a leg of the scheme to Parties the Coy in Con. Speedy into action from the halves + had arranged one = Bringing up ammunition by hand armour. The operation lasted from 10.45 AM to 3 PM. thereafter lost RS.	
"	20		The Coy turn out paraded Parade 8.30-12.30PM. for instruction on G.R. turn limber + Loco Armour, + forming up Barrage fire to lose on a given area. Afternoon:- Recreational Training. The remaining section	

T2134. Wt. W708—776. 500000. 4/15. Sir J. C. & S.

Army Form C. 2118.
95

WAR DIARY
or
INTELLIGENCE SUMMARY.
(Erase heading not required.)

Instructions regarding War Diaries and Intelligence Summaries are contained in F. S. Regs., Part II. and the Staff Manual respectively. Title pages will be prepared in manuscript.

Place	Date	Hour	Summary of Events and Information	Remarks and references to Appendices
WATERDAL	Co B 20		We attached to HERTS Regn. LF on Rail in a battalion Scheme. Weather changeable. R.S.	Ref. MAP HAZEBROUCK
SALPERWICK	21		The Coy marched to new camp area avit Billets ST PERWICK leaving Start Point at 7 EVEL CROSS LUMBRES 12 noon. arrived SALPERWICK 6 pm. weather rainy R.S. no one fell out.	HAZEBROUCK 5A
"	22		The Coy paraded 9 am for Squad drill & musketry Rifle & 7 Officers reconnoitred new training ground. K.R.	"
"	23		Weather load, rainy. The Coy marched to training Ground for instruction a training in the full Packs & accelery drill, use of Sling, Semaphore 8.30 am to 12.15 pm. In the afternoon Section & Platoon Retirements training. The training ground is 2 1/4 hours march from Billets. Capt. E.A. Cloke proceeded this morning to the lay to take up the position of 2nd in M.G. Officer 2nd Lieut Allington taking over the command so acting C.O. Weather good.	"

Army Form C. 2118.

WAR DIARY
or
INTELLIGENCE SUMMARY.
(Erase heading not required.)

Place	Date	Hour	Summary of Events and Information	Remarks and references to Appendices
Halfpenny	24		Sunday. Coy paraded at 9 A.M. for inspection. Roman Catholics paraded for Mass and Halfpenny Parish Church at 10 A.M. Weather Good	Cf. Map Halfpenny S.A.
"	25		Coy paraded 8.30 am – 10.30 am & carried out the drill in the vicinity of Bree's 5 Rectifying Stoppages, Semaphore & Map Reading. At 11 AM the Coy fell in & paid a parade to a training ground for the doll. Practice Unit Recognition, Troop's Movement & Action in attack & open of practice with Pack to celery Leaving for the return to Bellas at 4.30 AM, a two hour march. Weather good.	"
"	26		Coy moved off for training ground at 8.30 AM for training until 1 P.M. The following subjects covered 1st Lewis machine Pack loading Drill – Indication & Recognising Range Finding, A conformation filler of Pack Saddle Drill was introduced & given by H. Brigadier-General E.H. c/o Bellingham, 5 P.M – 5.30 P.M Lecture on cleaning of next days work & inspection of Anti-Gas Appliance. Weather unsettled.	"
"	27	8.30AM to 10.30AM	Coy paraded for Semaphore & Map Reading (including Laying gun by compass on a given spot). Those who have not fired a	"

WAR DIARY
or
INTELLIGENCE SUMMARY

Army Form C. 2118.

Army Form C. 2118.
No. 97
MACHINE GUN CO[Y]

Instructions regarding War Diaries and Intelligence Summaries are contained in F.S. Regs., Part II. and the Staff Manual respectively. Title pages will be prepared in manuscript.

(Erase heading not required.)

Place	Date	Hour	Summary of Events and Information	Remarks and references to Appendices
Saperwich	27		another course marched to the range under 2/Lt Hanley & 2/Lt Davies & carried out firing practice until 3 pm, having moved off at 12.30 pm. The remainder of officers under their Section Officers arranged guns from 1 pm to 3 pm. Weather unsettled.	Ref. Map. Hazebrouck 5A French
Saperwich @ Camp A.30.d.05.56	28		The Coy fell in at 9.45 AM ready to move off at 10 AM. Drew full marching order. They marched to St Omer a distance close to 10 km when they detrained & marched to C camp (Map Ref. A.30.d.05.56 28ult) arriving about 8 pm. No one fell out. Weather fair during the day, rich a violent rain & thunderstorm shortly after arrival.	Ref Map Hazebrouck 28ult Ed 6.A "
Canal Bank	29		Relieved the 117th bay in the Hill 70h Sector. 3 Sections in the line & one in reserve in the Central Brigade. Pluton taken over out Zouave Villa, one Wilson Ra Belle Alliance. Will Officers Tommy No 2, Three commanders Bulge Trench, Wilson Farm No 5, Inch Farm La Brique. Relief carried out satisfactorily & complete by 3 AM before the weather good.	
"	30		Situation Section out of the line & civilian carried out anti-gas drill in the morning & gun cleaning. There was a considerable amount of shelling around men Hill 70 between	

Army Form C. 2118.

No. 95

MACHINE GUN CO.

WAR DIARY
or
INTELLIGENCE SUMMARY.
(Erase heading not required.)

Instructions regarding War Diaries and Intelligence Summaries are contained in F. S. Regs., Part II. and the Staff Manual respectively. Title pages will be prepared in manuscript.

Place	Date	Hour	Summary of Events and Information	Remarks and references to Appendices
Canal Bank	8.0		4 one man was wounded at Tank Farm. The men of the H.Q. dug out on the Canal Bank were also shelled & two men were wounded. Weather good	French Relief. 25/W/2 Ed S A

Lieut. ???? ???? 118 M.G.Cy

M.C. 15

CONFIDENTIAL

War Diary

of

118th Machine Gun Company.

From – 1st July, 1917. – to – 31st July, 1917.

(Volume II)

WAR DIARY
or
INTELLIGENCE SUMMARY

Army Form C. 2118.

118TH No. 99

Place	Date	Hour	Summary of Events and Information	Remarks and references to Appendices
Coy. H.Q. Canal Bank Hill Top Section	1.7.17		Shelling continuous all day about Hill Top, No.3 Brew Farm, Zouave Villa, La Belle Alliance & Line Wilson. Contact aep to Brew Farm Shewan. Chiefly 5.9 & 4.2.	MAP REF. Argulen 28NW2 Ed. 5A
		3pm to 4pm	About 40 4.2 fell in the vicinity of Wilson Farm. S	
		9pm	11 of the same shells fell 75 x to 100 x behind the section.	
		9.30pm	Vicinity of dug-out at Threadneedle Street shelled with 12 5.9 & several H.E. shrapnel no damage done.	
			M.G. active against E.A. 1200 rounds being fired. Tracks & winch railways east of Mouse Trap Farm were fired on at night. 1500 rounds being fired. Walterjire.	
2.7.17			Intermittent shelling throughout the day at Hill Top, No.S. Brew Farm, Frost Farm. Coy. shot at C.20.d. 03.25. was continuously shelled from 1.30pm to 8pm & the dug-out at Zouave Villa was blown in about 2.00 5.9 & 4.2 being fired over. The team at Zouave Villa built a dug-out at Burnt Farm & occupied same. Walter fine. All guns & cans active against E.A. About 650 rounds being fired. Night firing 2000 rounds were fired in tracks & winch railway east of Mouse Trap Farm & Calvaire Avenue & tramways from C15.A70.80 to C10.c.10.30	"

Army Form C. 2118.

WAR DIARY
or
INTELLIGENCE SUMMARY.

(Erase heading not required.)

Instructions regarding War Diaries and Intelligence Summaries are contained in F.S. Regs., Part II. and the Staff Manual respectively. Title pages will be prepared in manuscript.

Place	Date	Hour	Summary of Events and Information	Remarks and references to Appendices.
Coy. H.Q. Canal Bank	3	4/m 55am	Hill Top N.3 continually shelled with 5.9 & 4.2	Ref/Maps
		3 am.	A few gas shells were put over against the same position Both lethal & lachrymatory	M/Palen
Hill Top		12.15 am	5.4.2 fell in close proximity to the dug-out at La Brique position the nearest 5 away	28 N.W.2
Sec 62		5 am	12.5.9 fell within a 50 yds radius of the Ridge. Trench gun. No damage done.	Scl 5A
			500 rounds trench S.a. weather fine.	
	4		Enemy artillery uncharacteristically active. Hill Top No S & La Belle Alliance being the only positions affected intermittently during the day. The trick works at the entrance of the shaft Hill Top N.3 was hulged in by shell fire making passage difficult.	"
			Shells used 5.9.4.2	
		10 p.m.	A.M.G. fired on Cone Willow- a.a. sniper was busy against this position	
		30 m	Weather Cool. About 500 rounds were put off by a.a.s.f. A but no results were observed.	
	5	1.30 Am	14,250 Rounds were fired on the enemy communication trenches, trench railways tracks	"
		6-2.15 am	during a raid carried out by the 1/6 Cheshires	Ref/ypre
			Enemy artillery actively greeted La Belle Alliance & Burnt Farm were intermittently shelled during the day with 4.2.a.	Ref/Maps
"		6.30 pm	12.4.2 fell about 100 x east of Our Boundary road & near the border (Arch Farm) St Julien	28 N.W.2 Scl 5A

T2134. Wt. W708—776. 500000. 4/16. Sir J.C. & S.

WAR DIARY
or
INTELLIGENCE SUMMARY

Army Form C. 2118.

Place	Date	Hour	Summary of Events and Information	Remarks and references to Appendices
Coy H.Q. Canal Bank Hill Top Lectō	5/7/17	12m	12 mins chopped in about the same spot. Night firing - carried out against Trenches Tramways East of Reuter Trench Farm & Roads & Tramways from C.15.c.70.80 to C.10.c.10.50 from token Farm No 2 Reuter Villa. 2000 rounds hung fire. Walker gave.	Ref Map Belgium 28NW 25/15A
	6/7/17		Intermittent shelling all day round Hill Top and La Belle Alliance cross 5.9	"
		9A.M.	9.4.2	
		9AM b	Threadneedle Street - 2 runs of dug-out heavily shelled with 5.9 & shrapnel about 1.0 p	
		10AM	bung hit men.	
			Nightfiring Tracks Achiet Kuldn Farm C.16.c.65.99 to C.16.d.17.28 junction of tracks & Tramway from C.15.b.57.40 to C.15.b.90.30 junction Tramways/Rw & light railway C.23.a.10.39. Calender Avenue Track & Tramway from C.15.b.70.80 to C.16.c.	
		10.50	10.50 pm all firing upon 3500 rounds hung fire. Walker gave.	
	7/7/17		Shelling continuously through-out most of the horizon with the exception of the section H.Q. at long street the junction St. Cnes Rent & Ross Farms were shelled continuously throughout the day C.20.a.50.56 also C.20.a.50.40 & 2 hung were chiefly during the night among M.G. which active enough the front at La Belle Alliance	

Army Form C. 2118.

WAR DIARY
or
INTELLIGENCE SUMMARY.
(Erase heading not required.)

Place	Date	Hour	Summary of Events and Information	Remarks and references to Appendices
Coy H.Q	7/7/17		C.20.d. above the ridge C.20.d.68.82 – 65.93, the fire coming from the direction of Hill Top	Hill Top/ Map
Canal bank			Night Firing Calendar Avenue Road & Tramway from C.28.b.70.90 & C.16.c.10.40, was fired on also C.16.c.65.99 & C.16.d.17.78 & C.15.b.90.30. 25.00 rounds were fired	28 NW Edn. 4
Hill Top Section	8/7/17		Weather poor	
			Intermittent shelling all day about Hill Top N° 8, Rafelle Alleman, Stirling Rowe & the Willows 5.9 & 4.2 being used. The gun emplacement at La Belle Alleman was blown up but	
		5 pm	The enemy's shell is exploded with 5.9	
		6-7 pm	Our A.A guns opened fire & brought down an S.A. which fell in flames behind the	
		10 pm	Enemy front farm heavily shelled with 4.2 & 5.9 some 500 shells also being sent over forward	
			shell holes & near to the emplacement & dug-out but no damage was done	
		12.am	Enemy M.G open busy on our field throughout the night on the forward & hill top but no occurrences	
	9/7/17		Weather good	
			Shelling quieter during the day, but the usual targets Boar Lane, Bear Lane & Beer	
			Avenue received some attention	
	"	11.30 pm	Enemy put up a very heavy barrage on our front line about Tenis Farm 2 chs or	
		11.40 pm	the right of the N° Clans. Own A.0.1 went up from the direction of these places	

Army Form C. 2118.

103

WAR DIARY
or
INTELLIGENCE SUMMARY.
(Erase heading not required.)

Instructions regarding War Diaries and Intelligence Summaries are contained in F. S. Regs., Part II. and the Staff Manual respectively. Title pages will be prepared in manuscript.

Place	Date	Hour	Summary of Events and Information	Remarks and references to Appendices
Coy. H.Q. Canal Bank	9.7.17	11.40pm	The Lne William gun fired 30 rounds on M.6.A.01 line. Enemy barrage duel away about 20 rounds later. A great many T.M. were used.	Ref. Map 1/10,000 27 NW 2SW
Hill Top Huts.			Enemy M.G. and S.A. Belle Alliance opened during the night. 50 rounds were fired in S.A. gun & 2 M.G. fire observed.	
	10.7.17		All the firing practically fire trembling all day.	"
		6.15 a.m.	About 20 T.M. shells were further opened the Rifle Trench harbour	
		6.7 a.m.	Gas shells were used against a B.gun dumps by Jeany but	
			A.C. gun fired 100 rounds ag Co. T.M. gun on Rifle Trench	
			Night firing 1.750 rounds on unimportant C.23a.15.24 C.23a.10.57 & C.24c.10 & 15 & 14 & 26.27	
			Intermittent shelling of Hill Top during the morning. Enemy balloon was	"
	11.7.17	9 a.m. 6 12 noon a.m.	C.21C.30.86 blocked up.	
		9.05 & 7.30 p.m.	Junction of Crug Street & Boar Lane by heavy shells with 4.2 & 5.9. The trenches in the Coy. street chipped during the day had its guns & Tripod carried out. They were got quickly on to evening. La Belle Alliance & Iron Bellew trenches also heavily shelled with 4.2 & 5.9.	
			Night firing was carried off round C.23 a.M.24.9 C.23a.10.67 — 30 rounds in type.	

WAR DIARY or INTELLIGENCE SUMMARY

Army Form C. 2118.

Instructions regarding War Diaries and Intelligence Summaries are contained in F.S. Regs., Part II. and the Staff Manual respectively. Title pages will be prepared in manuscript.

(Erase heading not required.)

118th No. 104

Place	Date	Hour	Summary of Events and Information	Remarks and references to Appendices
Coy. H.Q. Canal Bank	12/7/17	6.7am	Hill Top N/S shelled lightly with 4.2s. a blue was seen from their shelling of La Belle Alliance	Ref. M2C1/2 1 fusion 27 N.W. 25a
			A Coy Street during the day & night	
			Two shells were particularly noticed to burst with a huge flame when exploding. They fell near La Belle Allem. a came evidently from a French Mortar	
Hill Top Sector		1pm-3.30 / 7pm	Intermittent shelling of Threadneedle Street – Java Farm positions & various of shells 2,5, 4.7mm falling in the vicinity of Blue positions. 500 rounds were fired a count T.A. with the French that this of Bellem who turns last our Divisional lines. Weather good.	
"	13.7.17		The day was quiet in the whole except for intermittent shelling of Hill Top, No 5 & View Farm	
		10.30pm →	& La Belle Alliance. The area between La Belle Alliance & Laurel Villa was shelled with 5.9, 2.6.2.	
		2pm →	La Brique & district his was shelled in the building where the emplacement is situated but no damage was done K.I.L.	
				Weather unsettled
"	15.7.17		Relieved on the line by the 82 Coy M.G.C. with the exception of 4 guns under 2/Lt Davies which still occupied its old positions C.26.8, C.26.2, C.26.1, C.20.6. On relief reinforcements with a good clear of shelling, generally, relief was complete while R.A.M. proceed	

T2134. Wt. W708—776. 500000. 4/15. Sir J. C. & S.

Army Form C. 2118.

WAR DIARY
or
INTELLIGENCE SUMMARY.
(Erase heading not required.)

Instructions regarding War Diaries and Intelligence Summaries are contained in F. S. Regs., Part II. and the Staff Manual respectively. Title pages will be prepared in manuscript.

Place	Date	Hour	Summary of Events and Information	Remarks and references to Appendices
Bicourt			To Camp A30area	
A30 camp	15.7.17	5.30pm	Sections must the line provided to bivouac camp & refrained limbers	Ry Map
Bicamp	16.7.17		In the morning the men cleaned up & prepared to move Reft C camp to move to training area	Weather unsettled Sheet 2.5
A30 centonement			at 3.25 pm marched to Hazebrouck Siding C.17.d.5.5 entraining about 6 pm the train was	Sh 3 Ry Map
@17d.5.6			due at 6.30 pm but did not arrive until 11.30 pm.	Weather good Sheet 2.5
	17.7.17			Sh 3
				Sheet 27
Cog H.Q.	17.7.17		Reached Watten about 4 AM & marched thence to Moulle arriving 6.30 AM	Hazebrouck
Moulle B.0			The training area is commanded by this officer & the men descend into	S.A
3.2 – S.3		5.30pm	Section by C.O (Capt R Ellington) % the While coy informing of inclines	
	18.7.17		The Coy (less one section in the line) paraded at 8.15 a marched to its training area &	
			carried us practice in getting into artillery formation, about a two hours march	
			returning to camp about 3 pm. No 2 section under 2/Lt Culley attacked 16 Cheshire Regt	
	19.7.17		Coy paraded at 7.15 AM & marched to training area a conveyed tactical Scheme	
"			Mr & the hq & a trenches. No 2 section came back as under 2/Lt thomas	
			one & Lt under 2/Lt Cully to protect with 16 Cheshire. The Co. hunt shooting to hut	

WAR DIARY
or
INTELLIGENCE SUMMARY

Army Form C. 2118.

Place	Date	Hour	Summary of Events and Information	Remarks and references to Appendices
Coy H.Q.	19.7.19	9:30pm	a conference with the O.C. of the Coy. to discuss points of arrangements for the taking over of	Appendices 5A
Meaulte	20.7.17		[struck through]	
3.2.S.3	20.7.17		No 1 Section (10 Vickers) to leave 20.3 inclusive, proceeded by train to Albert	
			Coy. paraded at 7.15 AM & carried out the following parades:— (1) Company Drill (2) Musketry formations (3) Training in Lewis gun (4) Tactical scheme. Machine gun & Rifle about 2 pm	
	21.7.17	3.30/m	Inspection by Lieut J. Monro. I refer to Instructions for Musketry. 2 AM 9.14 Gas & pigeons etc. the plan for the photographic expedition to H.Q Section.	
"			8 AM 9.15 ditto. 9 proceeded to H.Q. Section to reconnoitre & at 7 am the relief of the following Coy. commenced with the 1st party of the Reserves — The coy. relieved 1" will be about 3pm. 9 pm the relief of the rifle section will be completed clean over states.	
"	22.7.17		Received by Bus to Z Camp. Timed to start at 1 pm but busses did not turn	
9 Coy H.Q.			all of 2nd Channel 7 Camp 1 am 23.7.17	Meaulte Woods
Z Camp/J H	23.7.17		9.30 & 10 AM Inspection of Gas helmets & child maskets &c. 10.10 on am Cleaning	
9.0.34			equipment 11 am 12:30 pm Cleaning guns & ammunition	Brusle peril

WAR DIARY or INTELLIGENCE SUMMARY

Army Form C. 2118.

Place	Date	Hour	Summary of Events and Information	Remarks and references to Appendices
Z Camp	24/9/17	8.45 AM – 9.15 AM	C.S.M. parade 9.15 – 9.45 Orderly-room drill 9.30 – 10 AM P.T. 10.15 AM to 11.30 AM Cleaning Guns & ammunition. 11.30 AM – 12.30 PM Mechanism & stoppages 2 PM to 2.30 PM N.C.O Class under a/R.C.M. To 2.30 PM 1 to 3.15 PM Officers explaining points in the coming offensive to this section. Weather good	Reg. Map 57D 528 howts 5A
"	25/9/17		Parades in the morning the same as on the previous day but there were no parades in the afternoon as it was decided to rest the men. The newly-advanced Yukon Pack was tested during the morning. The man to do so lifted C camp unsatisfactory. Weather bad.	
"	26/9/17		Parades same as before except that kit-fitting took the place of mechanism & stoppages during the first few days the attached men were specially instructed in loading & firing a single mechanism. Weather fair	
"	27/9/17		Morning parades same as above with Mechanism & Stoppages from 11.30 AM to 12.30 PM. The N.C.O class was again held from 2 PM to 2.30 PM a at 3 PM General Jellicoe & the 3/A Div. Art. lectured the Officers on the coming Offensive. Weather good	
"	28/9/17		Morning parades same as 27/17/17 Afternoon rest & preparation for move. The Coy. was put under orders to move at two hours notice at about 6 PM but this was cancelled at 11 PM Weather good	
2 Camp & A Camp	29/9/17		Coy marched to S camp leaving at 7.35 AM & arriving about 9.30 AM A great deal of carryall during the day in preparation for the Offensive.	Reg. Map sheet 28 Sec. 3

Order: The bu. to watch for the news of the day in preparation for the Offensive.

WAR DIARY
or
INTELLIGENCE SUMMARY.
(Erase heading not required.)

Army Form C. 2118.

Instructions regarding War Diaries and Intelligence Summaries are contained in F.S. Regs., Part II. and the Staff Manual respectively. Title pages will be prepared in manuscript.

Place	Date	Hour	Summary of Events and Information	Remarks and references to Appendices
S Camp				Ref map sheet 28 (43) 9
Canal Bank	30/7/17		Inspection of guns made a chill from 9 AM to 9.30 AM. After this limbers were packed. The men rested during the afternoon. At 9 pm three guns of No 3 section under 2/Lt ?? joined the 1/6 Cheshires for the offensive & moved with them to the line. At 9 pm 2/Lt Thomas with the guns of No 1 Sec and the 1/1 Herts did the same & the remainder of the Coy left at 10.40 pm reaching the canal bank at about 1 AM.	28/7/17 11.27 pm NB 2 28 5 a
Augurs a 2			Wellingtons shells exploded back leaving St Canal Bank at 5.40 AM	
"	31/7/17		Offensive opened at 3.30 AM. The guns each of Nos 1 & 3 sections joined 1 & 4/5 Black Watch on the left Hendou. Nos 2 & 4 sections formed with a battery V under Lt Woodley with 2/Lt Hull & Lt Lyles left the Canal Bank at 5.30 am to take up a forward barrage fire covering the advance of 118 Bgde see Appendix B. Nos. 1 & 3 sections on the advance with the infantry suffered severe casualties & have to return. No 4 section & half of No 2, with a few men of the other sections took up a position in Canteen Trench about C.17.b.65.15 & remained there. The remaining half section of No. 2 were caught by shell fire & suffered severely. Casualties 2 Lts Cutts & Lyles wounded, 2/Lt Thomas wounded & missing. 6 OR killed, 20 OR wounded & 16 missing. Total 3 officers & 45 OR. The offensive was hampered by bad weather & the ground became extremely difficult owing to mud. The rain continued all night.	See Appendices B

L.O. Rochdale Bt Major 118 Bgde MGC.

APPENDIX "A".

118th MACHINE GUN COMPANY ORDER NO.31.

B A R R A G E   S C H E M E for minor enterprise to be carried out by the 1/6 Cheshire Regt. on "Z" day. ("Z" day and ZERO hour to be notified later). Objectives - Caliban Trench & Support

NO 1 GROUP   Under 2nd Lt.H.D.Hanks.
    2 Guns STIRLING LANE (or BURNT FARM) :-
  (a) Search CALF AVENUE C.16.d.00.18 to C.16.d.18.28.
  (b) Traverse CALF RESERVE C.16.d.18.28 to C.16.d.34.15.
Guns to be used
  1 from Reserve and the gun in ZOUAVE VILLA position.

NO 2 GROUP   Under 2nd Lt.D.Moodie.
    3 Guns vicinity of **WILSON FARM**.
  (a) Search TRENCH AND SAP C.16.d.70.28 to C.16.d.94.42.
  (b) Traverse CALIFORNIA RESERVE C.23.a.12.60 to C.23.a.32.38
  (c) SEARCH CALIFORNIA AVENUE C.23.a.03.16 to C.23.a.32.35.
Guns to be used
  WILSON FARM N & S and LA BRIQUE.

NO 3 GROUP   Under 2nd Lt.W.C.Davies.
    2 Guns "X" line (C.27.a.75.45 approx)
  (a) Traverse CALIFORNIA RESERVE C.23.a.32.35 to C.23.a.50.00
  (b) Sweep ground behind MOUSE TRAP FARM C.17.c.10.45 to
    C.17.c.42.30.
Guns to be used
  Gun in "X" line and one gun from Reserve.

Guns will open fire at ZERO + 1 and fire bursts at the rate of 80 rounds per minute until ZERO + 6 when they will fire at the rate of 40 rounds per minute until the Artillery barrage ceases.

8 Belts will be needed for each gun but provision must be made for more should they be wanted. The Officers concerned will make their own arrangements about ammunition and indents for the amount needed to bring it up to strength must be sent in as soon as possible.

The synchronised time will be sent by Runner from this Headquarters at 9 p.m. on "Z" day. Officers concerned are requested to forward a watch to this Office before 6 p.m. on that day.

---o---

                        (Signed) S.D.RODDICK, Lieut.,
                            for O.C.118th Machine Gun Coy.

2/7/17.

Machine Gun Table.

Bty	Location	Firing		Targets	Rate of fire per gun
		From zero pluo.	To zero pluo		
V.	C.17.b.95.40	6.20	6.52	D.7.b. 50.40 to D.1.c. 50.70	3500 rds. per hour
		6.52	7.16	D.8.a.90.25 to D.1.a. 90.45.	3500 rds. per hour.

Vol 16

CONFIDENTIAL

War Diary

of

118th Machine Gun Company.

From 1st August, 1917 — to 31st August, 1917.

(Volume II)

Army Form C. 2118.

118TH

PAGE 109

WAR DIARY
or
INTELLIGENCE SUMMARY.
(Erase heading not required.)

Instructions regarding War Diaries and Intelligence Summaries are contained in F. S. Regs., Part II. and the Staff Manual respectively. Title pages will be prepared in manuscript.

Place	Date	Hour	Summary of Events and Information	Remarks and references to Appendices
Canteen Trench	1/8/17		Hiemi [enemy] shelling all day in this forward area increasing intensity during the night, a crump shell hit our advance by the German in late dug-outs on the bench, but they were unhurt & our	Ref. Map St Julian 28 N.W. Edn.
C.17.b.65.15			& there were no casualties during this day. The weather continues not so severe, becoming colder & different permanent. Ammunition & water were brought up. Mostly 5.9 used.	"
"	2/8/17		Position the same as on the previous day, but the shelling was more scattered & Hiemi [enemy] shot up different attacks but the attacks was unseen & was great to himself, there were no casualties. At about 10 pm the enemy used trench mortars with coal boxes. Also they had their machine guns covering the approach at Wallembock. Cap. redic. Heny. W.M.C. shelling on the vicinity of Canal bank. Weather improved.	
August 4th & Canal Bank W.	3/8/17		Guns & equipment cleaned in the morning. Afternoon rest. Weather good.	"
"	4/8/17		9.15 AM they were some details for advance for holding a duel with the hostile & ammunition equipment mostly mine objectives experience the wind is generally in the distance. Weather good.	"
"	5/8/17			
R.15.a.0.0	6/8/17	9.15-11AM	Same as for the 5 inst. At 11 AM the coy. cleaned up the grounds in the vicinity of the dugouts which had been allotted to us whilst billeted with previous fatigue. Weather good.	

T2134. Wt. W708—776. 500000. 4/15. Sir J. C. & S.

WAR DIARY
or
INTELLIGENCE SUMMARY

(Erase heading not required.)

Army Form C. 2118.

118TH MACHINE GUN CO.

No. 11

Place	Date	Hour	Summary of Events and Information	Remarks and references to Appendices
R20c5.4	10		At camp about 1 p.m. a draft of 5 men arrived from the Reinforcement Camp & also two officers Lt Mallen & 2/Lt Grand. Weather good.	Ref. Maps sheet 27 2" Ed
"	11	9-9.30am	Close order drill under C.S.M. Roberts	"
		9.30-10am	Inspection of all anti-gas appliances	
		10-10.30am	P.T.	
		10.45-1pm	Gun cleaning, belt filling etc	
		2/1.45	Recruiting to Williams arrived as reinforcements bringing total of Officers up to 11. 31 More men also arrived making the coy 3 o.r. in excess of establishment. Instruction - Firing order. Weather good.	
"	12	9.15am	Belt filling, gun cleaning etc.	"
		9.30am & 10.30am	Church Parade, a full muster of all ranks of denominations except R.C. 9 fewer. Will the reorganisation of the coy the officers distributed as follows:—	
		11.30am	No.1 Sec. { Lieut. G.H. Richards / 2/Lt Bonsor / 2/Lt Williams }	
			No.2 Sec. 2/Lt Moodie. 2/Lt Harrison.	
			No.3 Sec. Lt Hall. 2/Lt Grand.	
			Res. Sec. Lt Gawley. Lt Mallen	
			Weather good.	

Army Form C. 2118.

No. 113th
MACHINE GUN Co.

WAR DIARY
or
INTELLIGENCE SUMMARY.
(Erase heading not required.)

Instructions regarding War Diaries and Intelligence Summaries are contained in F.S. Regs., Part II. and the Staff Manual respectively. Title pages will be prepared in manuscript.

Place	Date	Hour	Summary of Events and Information	Remarks and references to Appendices
Proc 5.4	7/8/17	9.2 am	Coy marched off to Eecke area. Overfull marching orders from Flanertinghe to Caestre. Thence by lorries to Renescure arriving about 5 pm.	Ref Map Sheet 27. 2nd Ed & 27 N.W.
"	8/8/17	9 am	Inspection Skill & equipment of all O.R.	Ref Map Sheet 27. 1st Ed
		10 am		"
		10.30 am	Men cleaned up kit into a personal equipment	
		11.30 pm	Rest & Cleaning of gun cleaning with a heavy thunderstorm & rainstorm between 6 & 7 pm. Weather good	
"	9/8/17	9-9.45 am	Rest & Cleaning & parting up timbers	
		10 AM	Coy Paraded for inspection by C.O. after which it marched to the parade ground of Up 11 Herts for inspection by the G.O.C. Division. This parade was a dismounted one and taking part in the inspection of Ammonitory. Weather showery. The men on whole had turned themselves out in apparent'd comparisons with cat	
"	10/8/17	9 am - 6 10 am	Rest & filling & cleaning up gun equipment etc Parade for inspection by the C.O. preparatory to marching to the 11 Herts parade ground for inspection by the Army Commander (Gen Plumer V.C.B etc) Annual back	

Army Form C. 2118.

No. 112

WAR DIARY
or
~~INTELLIGENCE SUMMARY~~
(Erase heading not required.)

Instructions regarding War Diaries and Intelligence Summaries are contained in F.S. Regs., Part II. and the Staff Manual respectively. Title pages will be prepared in manuscript.

Place	Date	Hour	Summary of Events and Information	Remarks and references to Appendices
R 20 C 5.4	13	8.30-9am	Close order drill	Ref. Map sheet 27 Ed. 2
		9-9.30am	Conduct route march & information	
		9.45-10.30am	P.T.	
		10.30-11.30am	Bayfilling [Bayfilling]	
		11.30-1pm	Machine gun drill. The new chiefs are told in guard & seem to be laying	
			a also information. They appeared to be a very fair attempt from a good	
			[illegible] Wagon had previous advancement beforehand. Weather showery	
" Ridge Wood N 36 O.5	14		Coy paraded at 10.15 AM to march to Hells where it entrained for the new area on arrival	Ref. map Wytschaete 28 SW2
			at Kruibeke Comm. N 2 & 5.9 the coy detrained & marched to the billets in the [illegible] on the margin	
			this position was taken as the accommodation was better than that actually in the wood. Transport	alsr AP 110
			The weather was quite all day but there was evening rain set in & continued intermittently	sex 5 2
			throughout the night making the nose a general secrecy extremely muddy & difficult	
"	15	9-9.30AM	Close order drill. 9.30-10.30AM Gun drill. 10.45-11.15 am P.T. 11.30-12.30pm the J map & company.	Ref map Wytschaete 28 SW 2 Ed. 6 a.
		2.30 pm	Cleaning limbers.	
			At about 2.45 pm a flight of six enemy aircraft appeared high over the wood & camp, they were	
			vigorously attacked by our A-a guns & also by m.g. the shooting appeared extremely good & the planes	
			were seen forced to return. Weather showery	

T2134. Wt. W708—770. 500000. 4/15. Sir J. C. & S.

Army Form C. 2118.

WAR DIARY
or
INTELLIGENCE SUMMARY
(Erase heading not required.)

No. ......113......

Instructions regarding War Diaries and Intelligence Summaries are contained in F. S. Regs, Part II. and the Staff Manual respectively. Title pages will be prepared in manuscript.

Place	Date	Hour	Summary of Events and Information	Remarks and references to Appendices
Ridge Wood N5 c 0.5	16	9-9.30 p.m	Close order drill. 9.30 a.m — 10.30 a.m. Gun drill including the use of box respirators. 10.45-11.15am P.T. 11.20 am — 12.30 pm Instructions in bandaging. 2.3 pm cleaning & oiling Lewis guns. 2/Lt Proctor & Sgt Pannach returned from the Cytn Reinforcement Camp. Health fair but unsettled	Ry map Wytschaete 28 NW & Ea Ca.
"	17.	9-9.30 am	Close order drill. 9.30 AM — 10-30 AM Gun drill elementary & advanced, including 1/4 hour with box respirator. 11.30 am — 12.30 pm Use of map & compass. Weather good. 2/Lt Evans D.W. joined the coy from the base. Two A.A. guns were later of for the protection of the Div Transp(Amn) at N6 c.4.3. Two teams of N° 4 Section consisting each of 6 men & an NCO. placed the guns in readiness for action. The drivers up on the right, & left, a buwie shelters to lu in. It was arranged for two only to be covered but by the reclining position, the teams to lu in the girrage. the 24 horses only 16 miles were brought up upon the Transport lines a protective area tod. camp from aerial were arrangements made with the Brigade, to indicate the Coy movements in the event of an aeroar attack by the enemy.	"
"	17	9-9.30am	Close order drill. 9.30-10.30am Gp.musketry range card practical & gas helmet drill. 10.45-11.15. AM P.T. 11.30AM L.M. to fm. Measuring guns in different positions.	"

Weather good.

WAR DIARY or INTELLIGENCE SUMMARY

Army Form C. 2118.

Place	Date	Hour	Summary of Events and Information	Remarks and references to Appendices
Ridge Wood N.5.C.0.5			Cont-	Ref. Map Vijfschaete 28 N.W 2 Col 6 a (special)
Brig H.Q. at Bluff Tunnels	19.8.17		At about 4.15 p.m. one received sudden orders to relieve 119 Coy in the line No 1 & 2 Sections. All the camp at 6 p.m. with pack mules & the remainder of the Coy pulled out at 7 p.m. All the sections pushed to the Coy H.Q. at the Bluff & were taken on by guides to their positions. Bn. front line Belgium Trench Sheet 28. Col 3	(i.e. O.25-S1.Sp.)
			2/25 Brewe was O.R. relieved with 2.1.a. at the Transport lines. Owing to darkness & the difficulty of the ground the relief was much drawn out & it was 4 AM before it was complete. The concentration of Coy HQ was extremely difficult owing to the amount of traffic about.	
			There was not a great deal of shelling about the positions all whole during the day.	
"	19.9.17	2AM 6AM Pos 12.8.13 (I.36.a.50.15) (I.36.a.a4.15)	positions received a shower of shells in their immediate vicinity. 5.9 a shell an occasional shrapnel. One of shelling was also experienced around (B.9.10 &11) positions during the morning & also between the hours 1AM & 4AM. A gas shell attack the dugout & the occupants were affected slightly. This was section H.Q. O.5.a.2.a.5.b.	
			There was a certain amount of aerial activity during the early morning & evening but not much	
			range four guns	
"			At about 10 A.M a 5.9 burst in the trench just outside the dugout at no 3 position T36a.49.5/9.2/0" Hanks was hit in the head & side, one O.R being killed & wounded. There had been a general shelling of the position from early 2/O.Hanks took over no 123.13 positions with its shelled place	

Army Form C. 2118.

WAR DIARY
or
INTELLIGENCE SUMMARY
(Erase heading not required.)

Instructions regarding War Diaries and Intelligence Summaries are contained in F.S. Regs., Part II. and the Staff Manual respectively. Title pages will be prepared in manuscript.

No. 1/5

Place	Date	Hour	Summary of Events and Information	Remarks and references to Appendices
Bluff Tunnels Bgde HQ	19/8/17	9 AM	The Barrage guns known as B Battery were found not to be worked with trolleys as ordered at 8am 19/8/17. The removal of equipment and stores took several hours. The transport comp. O.R. trailers went down the line sick. Weather good	(a) Map (official) 1.1100vu - 2150v1 Reference frame sheet 28 S.E. 3
"	20/8/17		There was not a great deal of shelling about the position during the day in fact in most cases it was extremely quiet.	"
		1AM to 5:30 AM	During the night No 2 & 3 positions (21st Ramblers) received a good deal of attention & the embankment behind was heavily shelled, the nearest shell was 30 yds away from No 2 position, A 2 & 5. 9 inch H.E. shells used. No 1 Bde HQ the adjacent positions 8, 9, 10 were also shelled intermittently during the night but no damage was done & there were no casualties.	
		9:30 pm 15:11 pm 9 AM to 5 AM	No 1/2 position (21st Snow) was heavily shelled during the hours noted in the margin & during the latter part of the night was swelled a the day but it received some [illegible] mine [illegible] this nuisance was the only damage done was to refill a mens & officers also [illegible] the guns were not touched luckily. At about 3 O N [illegible] the day out a german trench mortar was found with a runic dug-out it was in excellent condition a [illegible] of ammunition with it. The Brigade was notified & the guns it is to be [illegible] as soon as possible Weather good.	"

T2134. Wt. W708-776. 500000. 4/15. Sir J. C. & S.

WAR DIARY or INTELLIGENCE SUMMARY

Army Form C. 2118.

(Erase heading not required.)

Place	Date	Hour	Summary of Events and Information	Remarks and references to Appendices
Coy H.Q Bluff Tunnels	21/8/17	5:15 AM	Our 2 & 3 Portions fired R.O.B. movement up near their trenches but there were no developments	Ref. Map Sheet — 11:10:070 - 28:20:1
	9.25/8/17 9		Upon enquiring it was found their some of the enemy had been seen on the ridge opposite.	Belgium & France Sheet 28 SE & 3
		4:15 AM	Both sides of the embankment were shelled heavily but their gun positions were not located, the enemy shell 28 SE & 3	
		to 5:30 AM	The day was quiet: O 6 a 5 ± 20 I 36 c 28 · 13 Map Ref. of Portions	Weather good
		AM – 5AM	There was little shelling in the vicinity of any of the other portions with the exception of No 17 There was little shelling in the vicinity of any of the other portions with the exception of No 17	
			O 5a 24·56 a a number of shells fell about here, but they seemed to be fired at random & did no damage. They seemed & continued 5·9, 4·2 & 7·7 cm also minning	
		7:30 pm 8:3 & 14	E. A. were active as usual in the evening & early morning A. L. V. G. patrolled the area 9.1 & 9.31 in the morning. They kept a sharp lookout & were fired at in the afternoon two of them came close to some of our wire but were driven off. The fired 25.0 rounds from	
		5:10 am 10:30 am	No 17 P.O. using tracer ammunition & the bullets were observed to be passing close & between the Piercers.	
			NOTE. There flares have invariably appeared at the same place & time since we came in, our flares nearly turn up about 6 am	Weather good
Coy H.Q Bluff	22/8/17		The day was quiet on the whole as far as shelling is concerned, the only shelling experienced being between O 6 a 57·20 & I 36 c 28·13. The shells used being 5·9 & 4·2, one fell in the doorway of the dugout at the latter spot but fortunately no damage was done & close 5	
Tunnels	23/8/17	9-9:30 1 pm		

Army Form C. 2118.

No. 117

WAR DIARY
or
INTELLIGENCE SUMMARY
(Erase heading not required.)

Place	Date	Hour	Summary of Events and Information	Remarks and references to Appendices
Coy H.Q. Bluff Tunnels	22/8/17		cont—	Ref Map. Revised 1:10,000 – 8110/1 Belgium & France Sheet 28 Col S
	22/8/17 & 23/8/17		a relieving native & line were no [cancelled]. Line was also intermittent shelling all day of the position at I 36 d 35.3 & chiefly this were obtained but beyond chipping the concrete & shaking up the people made no damage was done in this case either. This dug-out is an extremely exposed position, with the door-way a marked & directly facing the enemy line. This is of course in consequence of it's once having been an enemy clug-[out]. There was considerable activity on our front all day all over the sector, the enemy was active to but this unusual morning & evening festival were met by him & photos of pairs of each time chunks of M.G.s quickly in the morning & of the S.A. being observed to come down on & [within] in the enemy's lines	
		10.15 p.m.	An enemy plane was observed over the heads of the people at I 36 a 50.84, it dropped its gun lights when overhead & seemed to be trying to spot a battery about 150 N.W. of the position. Having dropped a white shower it [proceeded] over its own lines. It was picked out by two small lights under the wings.	
			Casualties — nil.	Weather fine.
"	23/8/17 & 24/8/17		There was no direct shelling of any of the gun positions during the 24 hours. Beaming were taken from No.17 position on flash near this 45° & 40 on the flashes of a couple of batteries	
			of area 115 B & 111 D. Gold respectively. In the latter case the guns appeared to be firing from the	

Army Form C. 2118.

WAR DIARY
or
INTELLIGENCE SUMMARY.
(Erase heading not required.)

Instructions regarding War Diaries and Intelligence Summaries are contained in F. S. Regs., Part II. and the Staff Manual respectively. Title pages will be prepared in manuscript.

118

Place	Date	Hour	Summary of Events and Information	Remarks and references to Appendices
Coy. H.Q. Buff Tunnel	23.24 Aug 1917		night above of wire during Thos P.12.a & P.18.b. A 77mm battery was shewing firing at S.14.A on line E N.E of Thourout about P.18.b 99.10 (aviation J.Bolting). There a good deal of aircraft activity during the day on both sides. A small machine (single seater aviation?) on a flight was brought down by an A.A fire (Archie) a man seen to fall from plane. (time each morning 23). Later in the morning an E.A was continually seen among own shrapnel M.G fire was brought to bear and hun asst had no effect. hun was observed on own Franzy own own M.G.f.	Ref Map Belgium & Tournai 27 Sept 3 ⑨ P[hase] 1:10,000 –8/50/1
"	24 & 25 Aug 1917		Cancelled. Weather fair. An extremely quiet day, the only shelling in the vicinity S.W [shrapnel] being 12.6.9 which fell near 1.35.a 72.82. Between 6.30pm & 7.25pm huts no damage was done. At 5.15 A.M. a hostile aeroplane crossed the line at a low height in the vicinity of O.5.a 24.5.6, 200 rounds were fired at it from two positions & the hare believed caused he showed signs between the planes, these bullets prove exceeding useful men against aircraft.	Weather fair
"	25 & 26 Aug 1917		A quiet day with no serious enemy shelling in the vicinity of own positions.	Weather fine

Army Form C. 2118.

No. 119
DATE

WAR DIARY
or
INTELLIGENCE SUMMARY
(Erase heading not required.)

Instructions regarding War Diaries and Intelligence Summaries are contained in F.S. Regs., Part II. and the Staff Manual respectively. Title pages will be prepared in manuscript.

Place	Date	Hour	Summary of Events and Information	Remarks and references to Appendices
Bluff Tunnels Coy H.Q.	25-26 Aug 1917		cont"	Ref Map 1/ Belgium France Sheet 28 Sol 3 B
		8.45 A.M	E.A. flying low approached the gun positions at I.35.b, 57.51.8, I.35.a.72.82. Both guns at once opened fire firing about 60 rounds each, the aeroplane	Sheet 11/10,000
Ridge Wood			approached to within immediately afterwards it is ascertained & came down in I.5 Central	-915D/1
N5cQ6 central		9 A.M	O.5.a.24.56. 9 two neat attacks were seen over O.26 & C.35 flying in a N.E. direction, they apparently	28.A.2
			were not large German guns	N.S.6.o.
			We are living in this enemy to the up lay a successful bombing attack by 11 pm Sol 6o	
			Capture to Ridge Wood. The march changed during the evening the ground	
			becoming extremely difficult. During the night received the day - no fire received	
			unnoticed by the noise	
		11 AM-12.30 pm	Cleaning up guns equipments etc	
Ridge Wood 87.21.4		2.30 – 3.30 pm	Gun cleaning & checking	
N5cQ.5 central	27/8/17		A quiet day taken up as above. N.C.O. & R.E. Plumber Received messages Walsh head	
		9.30 AM-10.30AM	Close order drill 9.30 AM-10.30 AM Gun drill 10.45 AM - 11.15 AM P.T.	
"	"	11.30 AM-12.30 pm	The 3 N.C.O. & compass 2.30 pm Inspection of Billets & Cook-house	
			Improvements were carried out in this camp. Weather continued bad throughout morning	
			but clearing up becoming fine evening	

Army Form C. 2118.

WAR DIARY
or
INTELLIGENCE SUMMARY.
(Erase heading not required.)

Place	Date	Hour	Summary of Events and Information	Remarks and references to Appendices
Redge Wood NSC OS	29/8/17	9.10 am	Close order drill 9.10-10.30 am Gym-drill 10.45 am-11.15 am P.T. 11.30 am-12.30 pm Lec F map & compass 2.30-3.30 pm Improvement of billets. Weather miserable.	Supplement 28.8.17 C.C 16.a.
	30/8/17		9-9.30 am Close order drill 9.30-10.30 am Lec & map o compass 10.45-11.15 am P.T. 11.15 - 12.30 pm Use of track academy 2.30-2.30 pm Improvement of billets Weather indifferent	
	31/8/17		The running machine & lorrry was branded and also the work of improving the camp Generally carried on. Lt Briand returned to hospital. The weather continued unsettled with very little sign of improvement	

A B Rochet Lt
O.C. 118 Coy M.G.C.

CONFIDENTIAL

War --- Diary

of

118th Machine Gun Company.

From 1st September – To 30th September 1917

Volume II

WAR DIARY or INTELLIGENCE SUMMARY

Army Form C. 2118.

Place	Date	Hour	Summary of Events and Information	Remarks and references to Appendices
RIDGE WOOD	1/9/17	9pm	Saturday. Coy carried on usual training till 11.30 am when	WYSCHAETE
M.S.C. 05'			Bn. worked parties the acting C.O. (Lieut. D. Forrest) and 2	28 SW 3
			other officers reconnoitred the SHREWSBURY FORREST sector	
			of the line. 2.25° Weather FINE	E6 & A
	2/9/17	10am	Boy, paraded for Inspection by C.O. the following O.R.s were	21st & DGKE
			inspected by the Medical Officer (D.R.O. 1039 Sermon Sources):	23 NW & and
			22011 Sgt. J. BAIN, 21965 Sgt. A.S. WEBB, 70281 Sgt. S.W. MORLEY	28 NE 3 hours
			Weather continues fine	
"	3/9/17	9am	Coy paraded and proper goods up for the line. Relief movement off	
			from RIDGE WOOD at 3 p.m. and and genl at JACKSONS DUMP R.7.8.c.6.1 at	
			5 p.m. by which time the 17th M'G.Coy. We came on relief was	
			completed by 9.15 pm. 2nd Lt. G.L. Wilson relieved 2nd Lt. Mackenzie will	
LARCH WOOD			3 other Coms & prints 2. Bn J.R. Scots joined the Coy from Divi	
19 a c 1385'			Hostile Artillery quiet. F.A.s showed considerable activity in the afternoon	
"	4/9/17		flying low over our lines. 250 rounds were fired at hand	
			Weather continues fine	

WAR DIARY
or
INTELLIGENCE SUMMARY.

(Erase heading not required.)

Army Form C. 2118.

Instructions regarding War Diaries and Intelligence Summaries are contained in F.S. Regs., Part II, and the Staff Manual respectively. Title pages will be prepared in manuscript.

118th
122
MACHINE GUN CORPS

Place	Date	Hour	Summary of Events and Information	Remarks and references to Appendices
LARCH WOOD	5/9/17		Hostile shelling slight. Between 6.30am & 7am 12.7mm shells fell near	ZILLEBEKE 28NW.1-4 28NE.3 (part of)
I.29.c.15.85			S.A. gun posts. J.25 c.4.5. Enemy aircraft showed great activity, flying low over the trenches & using their M.G.s against our posts & batteries. 4000 rounds were fired at them, at 9.15 am one of our S.A.A. Lewis B. planes was crashed by 2 E.A.'s in J.25 c. Whilst firing	
"	6/9/17	7.30am	10.7mm shells were fired at J.25.a.3 & 5 in returns. J.25.a ¢ J.25.c direct hits were observed	
			on the dugouts at J.25.a.6.8. & two hits on a.a. emplacement at J.25.a.4.5. Between	
			7.30 pm & 8.30pm a number of heavy H.E. (13in) shell in 685.a. b.d.f. no damage was done	
			& there were no casualties. 28 reinforcements to coys. & a will be sent that two	
			men was taken each in our lines, one was taken to Shrapnel & 3 on yesevalle road	
"	7/9/17		Relieved in the trenches by the 118th Bgd M.G.c. & proceeded to camp at Ridge Wood & spent	
			a cushy relief being shelled by 8mm shelling and gad gassing to the trenches and	
			transport circuit road. No shells fell on the camp. 8 machine guns	
Ridgewood	8/9/17		A quiet day cleaning up after the spell in the line pulling 8 surplus guns removed	Wytschaete
N.5.c.0.5			the weather continued good	28 SW 2
				Sh 6 a.

WAR DIARY
INTELLIGENCE SUMMARY
(Erase heading not required.)

Army Form C. 2118.

No. 123

Place	Date	Hour	Summary of Events and Information	Remarks and references to Appendices
Ridge Wood N.S.C. 05 9.9.17			Sunday another quiet day. Inspection by C.O. at 10 a.m. a uniform & Iron hat a Gun equipment generally under Section Officers arrangements.	Whitchurch 27 N.W. a
"	10.9.17		Commanding Officer saw the enlargements to Webb's gear. Reconnaissance Parties of Commanders and Section Commanders went to D.M.G.O. 2.0 to see ...	col b.a
"	11.9.17		dumped at T20d.50.60. No detail made. Carrying ammunition forward met with very slow progress owing to the Q.A.C. opening the advanced dumps. This case made the dump open until the morning of the 12/9/17 where	Zillebeke 9 27 NW 4 9
			1000 rounds were dumped at T20d.50.60 & T20d.90.20 with no accidents. The following casualties occurred.	NE 3
"	12.9.17		The morning saw man Pte Matthews sent to the & & still a list two wounded	Salsa
			The full names of the men were Pte O/H this date Military Cross Capt Wingfield. Lt Dawley C.S.M. Roberts D.C.M. Corpl Callingwood.	
	12/9/17		Nothing occurred during the day but in the evening bringing forward was furnished with 2.50 hours bring dumped at a dump ... 1.30 at 2500 the work was carried out with some difficulty owing to the relief of the division but luckily met with a shelling & no accidents occurred. Weather good.	
"	13/9/17		Day shown nothing at 4 pm every available man 9 & 2 mules left the camp to dump ammunition, above 70 hours were dumped at T20d.25. and 9.2.0 at T20d.80.30	

WAR DIARY
or
INTELLIGENCE SUMMARY
(Erase heading not required.)

Army Form C. 2118.

Instructions regarding War Diaries and Intelligence Summaries are contained in F. S. Regs., Part II. and the Staff Manual respectively. Title pages will be prepared in manuscript.

Place	Date	Hour	Summary of Events and Information	Remarks and references to Appendices
Ridgewood			cont-	Wytschaete
N31 O8	13/9/17		completing both OPs dumps. A good deal of shelling was experienced O 16	28 SW 2
			going on early evening & again later. Work was carried out without	SOT 6 a
			casualties. One man Pte Martin failed to return but was reported killed the	2 Ollebeke
			following day – out party which went to bring the body back when under	28 NW 4 &
			machine gun machine gun fire failed during the day but managed to do so during the	J 10 17
			evening. The C.O. Capt R Delvingler visited the OPs & has	NE 3
			recommended the party for bringing in the body	Caba
			minefield	"
"	14/9/17		Work of demolishing ammunition dumps carried on all available	
			men being used, a few cases of severe shell shock occurred but	
			there were no casualties	
15/9/17	15/9/17		Ammunition carrying & demolition continued, all dumps filled &	
			total 876 tons of Arty Ammunition were cleared. Weather good.	
"	16/9/17		Sunday Inspection in the morning. Men were in parade Dress in	
			good	
M36 &5	17/9/17		Commd to Westhouse Cabaret. We commenced Bivouacked the Shr 28	Bisecoino
			W Docks coad	Bisecoino
				France Fol. 3

WAR DIARY
~~INTELLIGENCE SUMMARY~~

Army Form C. 2118.

Place	Date	Hour	Summary of Events and Information	Remarks and references to Appendices
Mk.b.8.3.	18/9/17		Inspection by the C.O. in the morning of football match tomorrow	Shut 15 Belgium
			Michishi. Runs torno trek to Bridgewood arms Weather good	9 known
Matakuki	19/9/17		Arrived in camp in the early morning. Found that 116. 117 & 3 Coy had had return march to camp until the following day. A quiet day weather fine	Weather good
Mgbenbi	20/9/17		9. 9.15 AM Garrett drill – 9.15 – 9.45 AM Close order drill – 9.45 – 10.30 AM Musketry in stages 10.15 – 11.15 am Physical drill until C.A.M. 11.30 – 12.30 pm Bayonet in setting into a calm quietly to repel attacks 2 – 3 pm Bayonet fighting & N.C.O exam Bank & expired	Weather good
Mgbenbi	21/9/17		9 – 12 AM Inspection of the line bomfous made up during the afternoon of the afternoon companies each in miniature during daylight of Co. ship 10 miles supplies were left after truck was stuck in Bonit sand & no reinforcement the with were found to be very deficient & the Infelligence came	

WAR DIARY
INTELLIGENCE SUMMARY
(Erase heading not required.)

Army Form C. 2118.

Place	Date	Hour	Summary of Events and Information	Remarks and references to Appendices
G.25.B.5.1	22/9/17		A considerable amount of shelling was generally experienced throughout the day in the evening Pte W. Fordan (c.m.) Pte. suffering considerably Cpt. B. Shanhaw went down with shell shock & Pte Arnett concussed but no one was killed.	Zillebeke 28 NW & NE3 c 6 a
"	23/9/17		Reinforcements came to the units namely 10 men each for the 1/12 Bn. in the early morning & the 2nd "O". A great deal of shelling was experienced generally throughout the day but no one casualties were reported.	Weather warm. Weather fine
G.25.B.5.1 G.23.D.C.9	24/9/17		Which to the units as mentioned above. The whole Bde. was moved to the Menin Tunnel (Cambridge Tunnels) a reserve there. This was proceeded at & Fort made in the early evening by the enemy the preliminary bom- was & the units concerned successfully although some of the bombs had a severe bearing on the units.	Ilkenkin Tunnel
"	25/9/17		The day was spent in preparation for the forthcoming operations & the others were cancelled up as follows - A wilk of attacking battalions the 1/1 Camp & 5 Black Watch 2 in reserve and the 1/4 Black	

A6945 Wt. W14422/M1160 350,000 12/16 D.D.&L. Forms/C/2118/14.

Army Form C. 2118.

WAR DIARY
or
INTELLIGENCE SUMMARY
(Erase heading not required.)

Place	Date	Hour	Summary of Events and Information	Remarks and references to Appendices
J3 D.C 9.9	25/9/17		cont-	Zillebeke 28NW & N 23 Ed 60
			Two Companies advanced from Jeru sunken rd. The forward the centre of Le Chevalier Wood, the during the the of direction when they passed behind the hands of the Battalion commanders (Lt. S. the more forward under 2/Lt Timbs & Lt Walker) the battalions AG. 13 were members of both whom Rawlinson. The Barrage leaders were helping a rate on which a button was proceeding to J ?? ?? expert when upon ?? with which a shell a cc-??on wounded about 8 ?? the ?? ?? of a sudden ?? on the caused successfully	
	26/9/17	5.50 AM	On arriving in an ?? a n.w.n. can w with enemy the final attack in upon enemies position attacking held by machine all proceeded ?? ?? extreme gallantry dug in a ?? about 200 yards from the final objective with the battalion on going the look not ?? to each of ?? he however did not come off. The M.C. followed in rear to attack wight not reinforce them as a full
	31st		this found a muster them as a casualty of loss or one remembered the was cancelled two men were wounded. One team under Elle Hunks lost 16 dubitable in the whilst lent derived 16 116 Bgle. a our ?? received a visit from The Barra gives

A6945 Wt. W11442/M1160 350,000 12/16 D. D. & L. Forms/C/2118/14.

WAR DIARY
or
INTELLIGENCE SUMMARY

Army Form C. 2118.

Place	Date	Hour	Summary of Events and Information	Remarks and references to Appendices
J30 c.9.9.	26/9/17	cont-	We was carried out without a casualty but when it was over & the guns were being landed 2nd Lt. Rawlinson was killed outright. 2nd Lt Stewart and one man wounded & a shell which hit in the front of the gun pit was an extremely fortunate occurrence as 2nd Lt Rawlinson was a very fine officer & was a well liked much loved comrade who had under taken this dangerous service going the day but no more casualties & a new restaurant for the trestle was now ready.	ZILLE BEKE 28 NW & NE 3 & 6a
"	27/9/17		The day was quite peaceful & nothing of importance occurred as the enemy shell fire was subdued but although some enemy shells came & landed quite close by it was	
			not fired on 24 hours	
	28/9/17		The weather continued good & shelling was somewhat less than during the last few days although the men were turned out shells fell on the dark. Road lacked & consequently a few cases of shell shock were noticed remains slight - were shut up for some at 6C 6 3 c d.g.9. at 7.30 p.m. the two guns were ordered to relieve teams which were of cast and were cast - displayed each and every much excellent behaviour of our guns 2nd Lt Rawlinson was buried in the cemetery in & near opposite tramway at	
M.12 b.9.9.			the car proceeded & lost to Ouchy near Westoutre about M.12 b.9.9. Weather good.	Sheet 28 Belgium France Ed. 3

WAR DIARY
or
INTELLIGENCE SUMMARY
(Erase heading not required.)

Army Form C. 2118.

Place	Date	Hour	Summary of Events and Information	Remarks and references to Appendices
M13b.9.2	29/9/17	1 AM	Arrived in camp. A comfortable camp not too crowded. Oatmeal was issued greatly appreciated by all. Men turned in. Structure up provided until 3.30 pm. The dividing up included old drag equipment. 2 PM. Smith joined the Coy. 2nd M.E. Modern rejoined Coy and is at Command with the general.	Star 2J Return & Come
"	3/9/17		Sunday. Church parade RC at 11 am. 9.15 am Inspection by Officers. 9.30 am tea.	S/3
			Nothing of importance occurred. Battalion ordered in as but rest from working.	

L. H. Prochick Lt
Maj 115 Bn Mec
3/9/17

CONFIDENTIAL.

War-Diary
— of —
118th Machine Gun Company.

from 1st October to 31st October 1917.

Volume II.

WAR DIARY
or
INTELLIGENCE SUMMARY.
(Erase heading not required.)

Army Form C. 2118.

Instructions regarding War Diaries and Intelligence Summaries are contained in F. S. Regs., Part II. and the Staff Manual respectively. Title pages will be prepared in manuscript.

Place	Date	Hour	Summary of Events and Information	Remarks and references to Appendices
M.3.d.9.9. Fauquissart	1/10/17	8.30am	9am Inspection of arms & equipment. 9am & 10am Inspection of Billets.	Between 9 & 11 - Relief W.O.S.
			schemes carried out. 10.30-11.30am Range finding. 2-3pm Judging distance.	
			11am-11.30am PT. 11.45am-12.30pm Judo-cum-rest drill.	
		7AM	House Parade. 9.10am Coy being handed over to the reserve in billets. 10.30	
2/10/17			Section drill in coy & plat. 9.45-10am platoon drill. 10.15am Company training	
			(various) 10.30am orders. 11.50am inspection of arms (coy & plat). 11.45 - 12.15	
			9 Lewis MG & CAM. Rifle & MC Grenade 12.15-1pm. 1pm-	8AM
			2.15 Rifle & Bayonet Fighting. 2.30pm Cleaning of Arms.	
3/10/17		5AM	House Parade. Do. Gun. Cleaning & V.T. 2.30pm Cleaning & Inspection of arms	
			PT. 11-12 noon inspection of billets. 12-12.30pm lunch	
			House Parade 8.30-9am Company duties 9-10am Musketry course & Programme CT	
4/10/17		7AM	10.15-12.30pm Battn drill. 5.5.30 pm Lectures MOs & NCOs officers. Musketry competitions.	
			House Parade. The following Lectures were carried out when not	
5/10/17		7AM	being the range. L/Cpl Crabb Drill L/Cpl Buchanan of L/Sgt Rogers - PT.	
			Actions of sub-section (in march formation) - L/Sgt Angus Drill	
			No.1 Sec. Platoon Parade. 8.1am 9.2. 9.30 9.10. 3.10 3.30 7.30 evening Parade 7.45pm	
				Weather unsettled

WAR DIARY
or
INTELLIGENCE SUMMARY

Army Form C. 2118.

Place	Date	Hour	Summary of Events and Information	Remarks and references to Appendices
M13b 9.9 Tunker Camp	6/10/17	8.30-9 AM	Pt. 9.10 AM First half Bn on board SS of M Pan Capel under 2/Lt Williams. Second ½ 9.20 & ½ Transport 9.40 AM on ship — thereafter Lr. 2/Lt Walter. ½ W.L. Section Nor Bela 10 is Transport. Coy completely equipped ready to Embark ship is half-emptied.	Belgium transport 78523
"	7/10/17		Sunday - 7.30 am Horse Parade - 9.30 am Fall in Picket	
"	8/10/17	7 am 8.00 - 9 am 9 - 10	Coy placed in club & bathroom Horse Parade Bloc Balderkill Elementary training Michenham & Nephelpps Lecture Police Knowledge/ Fire discipline	Walt grumbling Allotter honey-pot &c Cannot but obtain Drenching skirling fire
"	9/10/17	2 - 9 pm	Morning programme continued, change work counter. White Nathan cause but embarking on green front tonight.	Weather myself

WAR DIARY
INTELLIGENCE SUMMARY

(Erase heading not required.)

Army Form C. 2118.

Place	Date	Hour	Summary of Events and Information	Remarks and references to Appendices
M51 9.9 Tonkin Camp	8/10/17 cont		The actual work recommenced the N.C.O.s who showed great intelligence in most cases. Applied also the men generally. The officers continued to lecture the ground re-room arranges told staff.	Appendix B menu attd.
"	10/10/17		Rouse Parade 7 A.M. Morning Programme a Range Work carried on. The majority of the new chaps behaved much in due to one day at the Malbed rest track.	
"	11/10/17		Rouse Parade 7 A.M. Morning Programme Range Work carried on. Range work completed & Taken up to see where the allowed was to fired as usual. Meets met to her firing.	
"	12/10/17		Rouse Parade 7 A.M. Range Work & Training Programme carried on. The weather continued fine with a little or no ground.	
"	13/10/17 9 A.M.		The Company carried out a route march with full pack. Duell first line transport about 9 miles being covered. Returning to billet about 12 noon. Reconnaissance party to be made to lift officers. The Officer No 10 in duty being informed once of himself to T.O. to recommend him. A month's leave to England.	

134.

Army Form C. 2118.

WAR DIARY
or
INTELLIGENCE SUMMARY.
(Erase heading not required.)

Instructions regarding War Diaries and Intelligence Summaries are contained in F.S. Regs., Part II. and the Staff Manual respectively. Title pages will be prepared in manuscript.

Place	Date	Hour	Summary of Events and Information	Remarks and references to Appendices
M.13.b.9.9	14/10/17		Sunday.	B.y.F
		9 a.m.	Bn proceedng by section to Stuberg & Childrens Bath, returned to camp Supplement	13 hrs
			N.C.Os came about 1.2 pm. The Officers at 1.45 pm. 12 Chaps up in rest camp	Sd 3
	15/10/17	7 a.m.	Cookhouse Parade.	
		8.30-9 a.m.	Trench Drill. 9-10 a.m. Lewis Gun Drill. 10-11 a.m. Musketry.	
		11-11.30 a.m.	Rifle Exercises. 11.45-12.30 Run with Major of 14th Regt.	
		12 - 1 pm	Dinner & Games. 1 pm Bn turn out including detail to learn & Sections.	
			In the afternoon a company event to the transport lines & one to No 2 section. One company between 9 & one acted - Nos. men each.	
			Practiced rifle exercises & bayonet practice in the intervals. The men each had a lay gun lesson between the Lewis Gun Sections. The men returned to Billets at 5.30pm. Prize money amongst each man - amount see regd	
			up by the latter	
	16/10/17		The Coy moved to another rest camp. The two newly arrived 9.30.	
			a.m. Marching to destination at 11 am arrived & had Dinner	
N.15a 8.4			That the camp to be let on & we had then arrived immediately	

WAR DIARY or INTELLIGENCE SUMMARY

Army Form C. 2118.

Place	Date	Hour	Summary of Events and Information	Remarks and references to Appendices
N150 c 9	16/5/17	conf.	The weather is 9 am were not suitable for an aeroplane to visit Mess. Afterwards a collision had to be built at the camp in every much combatable. The 2 men from the Battn. were.	B 85 Appx 25 Col 3
	17/5/17	7am	Force Parade. 8:30-9am. Close arms drill. 9.9.15am Rifle drill. Then repeated gas drill etc. 9:15-10:50am Musketry. 10:15-11:15am Aim drill. Elementary 11:30-12:30pm Instruction in bayonet fighting. Lt Bradley returned from leave. Weather cold.	
	18/5/17		Usual training programme carried out in the morning, rifle drill in the afternoon. A draft was issued with the Lewis Gun & ready for trip.	
	19/5/17		The morning was taken up with foot drill, also 9172 La/Corp. L. Weeding once behaved in the line. In the afternoon a writers had a chess match. Against a battery Artillery close by & mixed in a chess nearly good.	
Abingdon (?) Front	20/5/17		No 2 sections under 2/Lt Marshi & McDonald 9 & 184 R/S have been up to take up trenches between turns at 10:15 & 62, 9 & 50, 9.3 eight communication were. The usual training programme was carried out & the draft that can unloaded was placed in the afternoon. No 1 & 2 sections came under the O.C. 228 Trench Mortar purposes. Weather good.	observation Investigator

A6945 W₀W11422/M1160 350,000 12/16 D.D.&L. Forms/C₂/2118/14

136

WAR DIARY
or
INTELLIGENCE SUMMARY.
(Erase heading not required.)

Army Form C. 2118.

Instructions regarding War Diaries and Intelligence Summaries are contained in F.S. Regs., Part II. and the Staff Manual respectively. Title pages will be prepared in manuscript.

Place	Date	Hour	Summary of Events and Information	Remarks and references to Appendices
N15a 94	21/10/17		The Battalion carried out the time & details carried out the following programme	Belgium 9 Trenches
		9am - 9.45am	Inspection & close order drill	App 18 App 3.
		9.45am - 10.30am	Inspection of arms & equipment	
		10.30am - 11am	"	
		11.15am - 12 noon	Advanced gun drill	
		Afternoon -	Football	Weather good
			Sunday	
"	22/10/17	9.40am	Advanced gun drill including action, gun out, including action in & change of carriers.	
		1pm - 4pm	Conferences - Shrapnel - P.T. - Nothing noteworthy - Stages gun in trench	
			& comparison between schools - Packhorses by Quart N.C. Officers & field. Musketry non-m	Weather fine thus
		2.15am	Bn fell in to march to another camp. Weather very fine & warm on arrival.	
Albuera Camp	23/10/17		Coys advanced to 9.55 am. On entering new lines men took their kits & loading a car for all members of officers to contribute to the loss at M6 c 5-7	
M6 c 5-7			Served 9.00 Inspection & general cleaning up of new camp with Bn H.Q. Regr of Interior arrangements the back handwriting caught in. A lecture turned at a number.	

A6945 Wt W11422/M1160 350,000 12/16 D.D. & L. Forms/C./2118/14.0

WAR DIARY
or
INTELLIGENCE SUMMARY
(Erase heading not required.)

Army Form C. 2118.

Place	Date	Hour	Summary of Events and Information	Remarks and references to Appendices
Chippilly	23/10/17		Continued — Monday charging the half-limbers, which were taking rations to the	
Camp			mobile brk. district shell this morning by Jacks with no [?]	
M60.5.7			casualties to the echelons at the time, when our horses "stamp"	
	24/10/17		sent the next day to hang & way & had formed to be changed & [?]	
	25/10/17		[?]	
			A training programme of the usual description was carried out during the day. Stray horses [?] in the afternoon. Previous [?] from Brigade to [?] [?] shot without Stable lists out [?] Colours & [?] [?]	
	26/10/17		The morning was taken up with mechanical & [?] [?] made up all time on the boys. This [?] up [?] [?] [?] where under the [?] [?] of the weather was very [?]. In the evening a thunderstorm broke out with a little [?] [?] There was much rain but [?] [?] [?] [?] in this [?] [?] [?] & [?] [?] were issued 2/Lt W. Thorne returned from [?] [?] [?] [?] [?]	

Army Form C. 2118.

WAR DIARY
or
INTELLIGENCE SUMMARY.
(Erase heading not required.)

Instructions regarding War Diaries and Intelligence Summaries are contained in F. S. Regs., Part II. and the Staff Manual respectively. Title pages will be prepared in manuscript.

Place	Date	Hour	Summary of Events and Information	Remarks and references to Appendices
Chiswero Camp.	27/10/17		No definite information having occurred on account of the enemy having more but three hours had no observations known including the shelling shells decided increased to be lost by A.P. Wilson in M.6.b. Gen. O. proceeded to encounter the line. The Coy had taken up lineup at 6.30 a.m. returning about 2.30 p.m. Not a great amount of shelling was encountered.	60 &F Sept. 35
"	28/9/17		Sunday. There were during hrs of 24 hours there were motorcades right a church house on top. A bomb at 10.15 a.m. The Infantry & the Brigade proceeded up to look in the line.	
Chiswero Camp	29/10/17		Very heavy hostile shell 12.45 to noon on the line foreshore guns the 30.39 & 6.431 0475 Hps 3 guns each & 6 guns a battery had been letting off 6-9 to 8.2 0 hrs 22 NS 0 The hostile was even now light of the ground hundred of and 30.62 a bridge. There undoubtedly & became much of the ammunition in view. The infantry was tight. With the exception of some friendly with the between 6.15 pm. 7.15 pm with 5.9 m burst within the Casualties nil	
M.6.a.5.7.9. Dug-out of O. Hedge about 7 acres				

Army Form C. 2118.

WAR DIARY
or
INTELLIGENCE SUMMARY.
(Erase heading not required.)

139

Instructions regarding War Diaries and Intelligence Summaries are contained in F. S. Regs., Part II. and the Staff Manual respectively. Title pages will be prepared in manuscript.

Place	Date	Hour	Summary of Events and Information	Remarks and references to Appendices
Hellis	July 20/17	5:15 AM 5:15 AM	Enemy trench mortars active with 5.9 & 7.7cm but without serious damage.	GHELUVELT 28.N.E.B
			6.5 pm Enemy's armour-piercing shells struck three M.B. emplacements.	
			The main road between pillboxes 2 & 3. South of Road received a line	
			Relieved in the trenches by 9 Durham L.I. & this was completed by 1am	
			Casualties	
	21/10/17		9 trombones attached to the Bn. were away down to the trenches and returning were	
			during the march about four Rushes E.P.F.S Dump at 11:15 pm one trombone was hit by	
			H.E. Evidence a Pepper shower. Our casualties being three trombones hit	
			From 9th to 25 Hanover pts are reported while Regt. in trenches as follows —	
			Killed - Other Ranks 13 Officers — Wounded — Officers —	
			Other Ranks —	
			Casualties W.R. hand & R shell shock	

S. O. Lodwich Col.
11th Bn York

CONFIDENTIAL.

War Diary
of
118th Machine Gun Company

From 1st November 1917 to 30th November 1917.

Volume II.

WAR DIARY or INTELLIGENCE SUMMARY

Army Form C. 2118.

118th [Machine Gun Coy]

Instructions regarding War Diaries and Intelligence Summaries are contained in F.S. Regs., Part II. and the Staff Manual respectively. Title pages will be prepared in manuscript.

(Erase heading not required.)

Place	Date	Hour	Summary of Events and Information	Remarks and references to Appendices
Near Ypres	1/11/17	9am–10.30am	Our army M.G. fired at enemy body returning from Langdale Trench to dugouts. No information but no circumstances on Ghela. Hostile Battery caused to disappear. One hostile trench mortar fired 4334 50 60 other shelling 38. L 82.10. Very few men left & unreachable on M.a.p. C Long reconnoitred enemy vulnerable.	G. HELUVELT 28. V.E. 3 C.a.5.a.
"		4pm–9pm	reducing the Menin Road during the night. Our 9" how shells falling on the road. Slow Venues harassing enemy above.	
"			3 a.m. our M.G. party proceeded to new positions above there.	
"	2/11/17		At moment on arrival it showed 9'/m & 3.30am. Rockets fired. Mostly avoid enemy post as Lewis lines by machine guns. When lengthy Canadian movements to be noticed getting up to line.	
"		3am–7am	hostile action on the Anouristy. Used Wh.	
"		7pm–11am	No. 3 L.C. 25	
"		1.30am	evacuation	
"			Evans M.G. team left 6.2. C.S. on enemy M.G. not machine but & law above thi night from the ruined D.P. Pillbock Chateau & another team formy	

WAR DIARY
or
INTELLIGENCE SUMMARY

Army Form C. 2118.

118th MACHINE GUN COY.

Place	Date	Hour	Summary of Events and Information	Remarks and references to Appendices
HEDGE STREET	2/11/17		Cont— Inclined guns on the Menin Road. The guns were used to be employed in the enemy Road	GHQ LOVETT 28NE3 SQ3a
			About 1500-2000 rounds were fired on the enemy front line. Guns were reported to be engaging	
			during the night in the similar role. Harassing fire on enemy's day dispositions	
			About Nieuwkerke House sq. grid N 21 c 95.35. No casualties on day dispositions.	
			Casualties OR. Newman. Mitchell wounded by shell in the enemy	
			and individually practically all day through the night.	
3/11/17			Hostile artillery not active during the day, but lively at intervals throughout the night. Gas a considerable amount of gas shells being used. Our barrage battery carried out harassing fire on known targets on previous nights. Weather dull, cold, indifferent visibility. Casualties Nil.	
4/11/17			The day was quiet. The coy was relieved by 116th C.Coy. Relief started at 4p.m. and was complete by 6.30p.m. No casualties. Coy proceeded by lorry from Chippewa to CHIPPEWA CAMP and grateful the same lists on furnish. Weather fine, good visibility.	116 C.Coy

WAR DIARY
INTELLIGENCE SUMMARY

Army Form C. 2118.

Place	Date	Hour	Summary of Events and Information	Remarks and references to Appendices
CHIPPEWA CAMP M.G.A.S.C.	5/11/17		The morning was spent in cleaning up and refitting of kit and equipment. Lieut N.E. BEAUMONT (Machine Gun) Attd M.G.C.) awarded the MILITARY CROSS. Weather fine, but dull.	BELGIUM SHEET 28
"	6/11/17		The usual training programme was carried out. Weather showery	
"	7/11/17	7am	The Company went to Baths at WESTOUTRE. The usual training was carried out during remainder of the day. Weather showery	
		~10pm	A few bombs were dropped by E.A. in the vicinity of the camp during the night.	
"	8/11/17	2P.M.	The Company moved to new camp at N.5.d.9.9. This was a tented camp and the accomodation was not good. Weather fine in the morning, but rained heavily towards evening.	
N.5.d.9.9.	9/11/17		The Company landed for instruction in the morning. Remainder of day was spent in improvement of billets. Weather Showery.	
"	10/11/17		The Company left and for the line. The C.O. + 3 M.G. officers accompanied the POLDERHOEK Section of the line. Two guns of N°1 Section relieved 2 guns of 13th Company at J.22.a.A0.45.	GHEULVELT 28NE 3 & 6.A.

Army Form C. 2118.

WAR DIARY
or
INTELLIGENCE SUMMARY.
(Erase heading not required.)

Place	Date	Hour	Summary of Events and Information	Remarks and references to Appendices
J.14.b.35.90	11/4/17		Remainder of company moved up, reaching new eg. H.Q. J.14.b.35.90 at 7.30 AM. No 4 Plation relieved 4 guns of 205th M.G.Cy in Rarge position near NORTHAMPTON FARM. No 2 Section relieved 4 guns of 13th M.G.Cy at J.22.a.33.55, J.16.c.60, J.16.c.73.18, J.14.c.72.45. No 3 Section and 2 guns of No 1 Section relieved 6 guns of 117 M.G.Cy at the old positions on and north of the MENIN ROAD. The relief was successfully carried out without casualties. Weather fine.	G.H.Q. DIARY Z.S. No 3 SL 6A
"	12/4/17		Between 8-9.15 AM enemy shelled front line in J.16.c with heavy shells. During the remainder of the day hostile artillery was active against trenches and small craters. Hostile M.G.'s were very active from neighbourhood of POEDERHOEK Ch[ateau] in the front line, active against our front line. Weather fine.	
"	13/4/17		Hostile artillery active during the morning, but nature during remainder of the day, against trenches. No 4 Platoon relieved No 2 Section in the front line. 2 guns of No 3 Section relieved 2 guns of No 1 Section at J.22.c.40.45	

WAR DIARY
or
INTELLIGENCE SUMMARY.
(Erase heading not required.)

Army Form C. 2118.

Place	Date	Hour	Summary of Events and Information	Remarks and references to Appendices
J14C3590	14/4/17		Enemy raided our front line in J16C about 1 p.m. and succeeded in effecting an entrance by means of festoon H.Q. under cover of a barrage of Trench Mortars and Rifle Grenades. He was driven off by our M.G. & Lewis gun fire. Casualties 1 R.&F. wounded by Grenade, 1 who wounded by sniper. The N.C.O. could not be evacuated & afterwards died. Everything was fairly active against the remainder of battn. With the Bns. 64 men were allotted to FA with Twelfth Bgde.	C. HEZOUST 28 N.E.3. BL.64.
"	15/4/17	5.22.a.m.	Enemy made an attack at 5.35 a.m. against our portion. On 2 M.G's were standing to, and enough of the enemy at about 30 yds range infantry being somewhere in him and driving him back. The attacking party were about 100 strong. 1 Pte. W.Bell and Cpl Holmes were killed whilst accompanying the ground N. of REUTELBEEK. We were relieved during the night by 119 M.C.My and proceeded by lorry to CHIPPEWA CAMP, Winter circle.	

WAR DIARY
or
INTELLIGENCE SUMMARY.
(Erase heading not required.)

Army Form C. 2118.

118TH

No. ....

DATE ....

Place	Date	Hour	Summary of Events and Information	Remarks and references to Appendices
CHIPPEWA CAMP M6a5.6	16/11/17		The day was spent in rest and cleaning up. Walking out.	B&G.IVM S4E5E29
	17/11/17		Kit inspection and cleaning of Gun equipt. occupied the morning. The afternoon was spent in recreational training.	
	18/11/17		Coy was billed in the morning and spent the afternoon in Ypres itself viewing the enemy. Weather fine.	
	19/11/17		The coy relieved the 117 MG Coy in the POLDERHOEK SECTION going to their position on before. Relief was complete at 9.15 P.M. Casualties 1 o.r. killed and 1 o.r. wounded. Coy HQ. MG Gun in MENIN ROAD. Hostile M.G's were very active. Wires went to all Guns. Hostile artillery quiet except slight activity again trenches. Gentle Gun + rifle shell.	CHEEWECT SECTION 28 NE 3
JY249	20/11/17			
	21/11/17		Artillery again quiet. Our tanks at J22a #3 fired with effect in enemy movement in J23a etc. + silenced 9 heavy trench mortar Rifles. Bad visibility.	
	22/11/17		Be co-operated from Barrage Position in a gas projection against	

Army Form C. 2118.

WAR DIARY
or
INTELLIGENCE SUMMARY.
(Erase heading not required.)

Instructions regarding War Diaries and Intelligence Summaries are contained in F. S. Regs., Part II. and the Staff Manual respectively. Title pages will be prepared in manuscript.

Place	Date	Hour	Summary of Events and Information	Remarks and references to Appendices
J14 & J9	21/11/17		GHELUVELT. Firing in MENIN ROAD from J22 4.1 - J29a 15.75 Hostile artillery active.	GHELUVELT 28NE3
"	22/11/17		On turn at J22 4.3 fired on enemy withdrawing from his advanced posts at dawn. Hostile artillery active.	"
"	23/11/17		Artillery activity increased owing to good visibility. Enemy H.Q. at J22 & J21 was shelled throughout the day. Active activity was noticeable - two of our planes visible but none seen over Coy H.Q.	"
"	24/11/17		Hostile artillery was very active, frequely in reply to bombardment carried out by un Heavy Artillery. Enemy hostile the day. Weather fine, but windy & rainy.	"
"	25/11/17		Hostile artillery active throughout the day. a considerable slackening in our Hostile Barrage. Rifle or Weather continued fine, but inclined towards rain.	"
"	26/11/17		Day quiet. 16 Coy wounded with enemy by a Coy SEAFORTHS who attempted a raid successfully with no casualties thus inflicted.	"

WAR DIARY
or
INTELLIGENCE SUMMARY
(Erase heading not required.)

Army Form C. 2118.

Place	Date	Hour	Summary of Events and Information	Remarks and references to Appendices
			CHELUVELT	
J19b A.6	26		During the day moved down the line by light Railway to Infantry	27 NE 3
Dickebush			Barracks. Showers in am.	Belgium
Camp	27		Left entrainee at Ouderdom about 3.30pm for billets in the Reninghelst	9 Frome Sheet 23
G19a.6.6			advanced area. Ordnance etc. members about 4 kilos W. of billets. Good	16 o.c. 27
Q15.b 0.6.			trams in 7 and 8 huts. There is a living accommodation in farm	
			buildings with the Remt. S. Battalion nearer. Weather wet.	
Q15.b 0.6	28		Occuring trades from 6.30 a.m. the morning was spent in cleaning up	April 27
			the guns, ammunition belts, & the various equipments. The men enjoyed	
			themselves having a good bath.	
			In the afternoon an equipment was issued on the recommendation of	
			adm 16 after 2 am equipment inspection. Orders C. drill & firing	
			techniques weak upon policy to be carried on tomorrow. The CO. Coll & Sharpes	
			Inc ldt. and Lewis Gun demonstration at the Tempest. Weather extensive	
	29		General Rearrangement was carried out during the morning a good drill	
	30		in the afternoon. The lines as unfit for 3000 offices & an NCO. from the Div	
			Gas School. The Ordnance funds Tempest. Weather fine throughout but showery	
				to rain in the afternoon.

CONFIDENTIAL.

War Diary

— of —

118th Machine Gun Company

from 1st December 1917 to 31st December 1917.

Volume II.

Army Form C. 2118.

No. 14-1
DATE:
MACHINE GUN COY.

WAR DIARY
or
INTELLIGENCE SUMMARY.
(Erase heading not required.)

Instructions regarding War Diaries and Intelligence Summaries are contained in F. S. Regs., Part II. and the Staff Manual respectively. Title pages will be prepared in manuscript.

Place	Date	Hour	Summary of Events and Information	Remarks and references to Appendices
Eerke	Aug 1/17		The whole of the morning was taken up with baths + the cleaning up of the Battalion lines. A Church parade + a short route march was held in the afternoon.	Ap 1/17 Col 2
O.15.cend			Inspection of Base Kit Bull to be carried out on 10th inst.	
"	2/12/17		Inspection of hostile 2 Aircraft gun sites. No ground observation of the hostile. Sunday Church parade for Methodists & Church of England. Brigade service for Presbyterians. No Campbellem were appointed. Mr Corrigan Welfare party. No Coy afternoon football.	
"	3/12/17		The following programme was carried out from 9am–1pm. Bomb inclin, Close Order Drill, Coy Drill, Gun Drill, PT & Lewis Gun. In the afternoon, Inter Pln. Knockout Football. 2/Lt Chalmers received Orders & Sick at No. 36 C.C.S. of Trench Feet. Lieut Wilson remained in command.	
"	4/12/17		Morning – Observation Drill, gun sites, Musica etc. Afternoon PT Lewis Gun & Rifle Practices, Drill etc. Inter Coy Football Final.	Feared out party
"	5/12/17		Above Coy programme + the above are carried out a Coy new one place in the afternoon. Huns very active + carried out 6 No 382 shelving us in the afternoon. An artificial barrage shell fell in + at 10am chiefly rear of town.	Weather bright + sunny. Ammunition carrying Coy

Army Form C. 2118.

WAR DIARY
or
INTELLIGENCE SUMMARY.

(Erase heading not required.)

No. 118TH
MACHINE G
DATE 1.4.8.

Place	Date	Hour	Summary of Events and Information	Remarks and references to Appendices
Sector Onsur	5/2/19 (Wed)		Under the C.A.M. & a class for all N.C.O.s under the road Sgt Wa also continued. Men 3/7	1 & 2
Q.10 Central			him 3/4 hour m all working days when possible. The idea being not to get firemen hard.	
"	6/2/19		Usual programme Instructional agreement in the afternoon. Whole day.	
			2 in OR and including a 1/2 to a hour pair of Ml/o a.m. for a wiring comp. In the morning being shown from his hose, he was caught up with the wire and after showing but he very two were not my gunners & he must than this.	
"	7/2/19		New chaff party, A general clean up to order. Weather cool to ground hard fog held 3/2/19. The thermometer was at 1.30 a.m. Lieut Manly my will not half after 7.45 am in camp out. Hostling all bo off till full attained noise of 10 am. The weather remained good.	
"	8/2/19		The Company paraded for inspection at 7.0 am and moved off at 7.45am be marched to GODEWAERSVELDE where we entrained at 12.30 pm. There were numerous stops during the journey, and we arrived at NIELLE ET BROUCQ at 7 pm where we detrained and marched to WATTERDAL. Weather - Bright but frosty.	

Army Form C. 2118.
No. ....1149..........
DATE ....

MACHINE G... No. ...

WAR DIARY
or
INTELLIGENCE SUMMARY.
(Erase heading not required.)

Instructions regarding War Diaries and Intelligence Summaries are contained in F. S. Regs., Part II. and the Staff Manual respectively. Title pages will be prepared in manuscript.

Place	Date	Hour	Summary of Events and Information	Remarks and references to Appendices
WATTERDAL	9/12/17	—	Inspection at 8.30 am, moved off at 8.45am. The Bn. marched to BRUNEMBERT, arriving there at midday. Weather - slight snow and very cold.	HAZEBROUCK &?
BRUNEMBERT	10/12/17		The usual programme of work was carried out including Close Order Drill, Gun Drill, Revolver Drill and Physical training. Football in afternoon	CALAIS
	11/12/17		In the morning the programme was Close Order Drill. Once with Box respirators & P.H. Helmets. Mechanism and stoppages, Physical training and Indication & Recognition of targets. Recreational training in the afternoon	
	12/12/17		During the morning the company carried out the usual programme of work. [Weather - clear frosty] 2/Lieut D Woods rejoined the Coy from leave. Weather - fine.	
	13/12/17		The usual programme was carried out in the morning. (Weather fine).	
	14/12/17		Usual Programme in morning. Football and Cross country running in afternoon 2/Lieut Williams proceeded on leave to U.K. Lt Hall attended continuation class over Pte Reid, as prosecutor.	
	15/12/17		In the morning was general cleaning up and washing of limbers in preparation for inspection by the Divisional General.	

Army Form C. 2118.

WAR DIARY
or
INTELLIGENCE SUMMARY.
(Erase heading not required.)

Place	Date	Hour	Summary of Events and Information	Remarks and references to Appendices
BRUNEMBERT	16/12/17	—	Inspection by CO ½ church parade in the morning. In the afternoon we played "C" Coy ½ Lincs (at football) on our own ground. Result fine. Goals 2 to "nil" in our favour. Weather — fine but frosty.	Sheet Calais 13
"	17/12/17	—	Morning programme — Inspection and close order drill. Inspection of arms Appliances — Special instruction in rolling harrying blankets on the march. Mechanism of Lugingers and Physical training. Promulgation of the Sentence of Pte Reid (28 days F.P. No 2 & 80 day's pay Rn). Pte Richardson received news that his father has been seriously wounded & was lying at Rouen. He went there found his father had already passed away. Weather — Cloudy even.	
"	18/12/17	—	The usual programme was carried out in the morning. Afternoon football. Weather - Intermittent rain	
"	19/12/17	—	In the morning the Divisional General inspected the Coy together with the ½ Herts. In the afternoon we played the 4 Coy ½ Herts. Result. M.G. 4 goals. HERTS 1 goal. Weather. frosty.	

Army Form C. 2118.
118TH
No. ...../5./
DATE ....
MACHINE GUN

WAR DIARY
or
INTELLIGENCE SUMMARY.
(Erase heading not required.)

Instructions regarding War Diaries and Intelligence Summaries are contained in F. S. Regs., Part II. and the Staff Manual respectively. Title pages will be prepared in manuscript.

Place	Date	Hour	Summary of Events and Information	Remarks and references to Appendices
BRUNEMBERT	20/12/17	—	The usual programme of recreational training in the morning & in the afternoon. Weather — heavy snowstorm	CAZ615/2
"	21/12/17		The morning was taken up with Gun Drill P.T. and taking up positions in the open. Weather — snow.	
"	22/12/17		In the morning the usual programme was carried out. Arrival of 3 Sergeants from base efwm upon from 157 & Coy. The above were posted. In the afternoon the Brigade cross country run took place which Rutter coming in fourth fifth. Weather — snow.	
"	23/12/17		An easy day. C.O's Inspection. Church Parade. Went to the Coy's. In the afternoon we played B. Coy. The Cards The Cards walked off the field as we scored the winning goal. Result 2 goals to 1 for us.	
"	24/12/17		The usual training during the day.	
"	25/12/17		Christmas Day. A dinner was provided for the men by the Company Officers. This was a huge success	

WAR DIARY
or
INTELLIGENCE SUMMARY.
(Erase heading not required.)

Army Form C. 2118.

Place	Date	Hour	Summary of Events and Information	Remarks and references to Appendices
BRUNEMBERT	26/12/17	—	The usual training programme was carried out. Inoculation of men who hadn't been done. Meat & biscuit ration of iron rations were counted. The men received extra meat. Weather – Very heavy snow storm	C2 27/5/13
"	27/12/17	—	The morning was taken up by the usual programme. In the afternoon the Divisional Cross country run took place. Heavy snow covering the day. Forster fell off the horse	
"	28/12/17	—	General preparation for the move	
"	29/12/17	—	We moved off from Brunembert at 9.30am & marched to WATTERIDGE [Hesdigneul?]. Transport moved off to join the Column	3°
WATTERDAL	30/12/17	—	Move cancelled. Spent the day at WATTERDAL. Weather dull & cool	
"	31/12/17	—	Moved off at 10am & marched to LART	
LART	1/1/18	—	Moved off from LART at 12.45am & marched to HAZEBROUCK. Detrained at St Jean at Haze. When we entrained as Advance Guard	
			Billeted in support area at Canal Bank	

ork van Hyst

CONFIDENTIAL

War Diary

of

118th Machine Gun Company.

from 1st January 1918.
to 31st January 1918.

(Volume II)

Army Form C. 2118.

WAR DIARY
or
INTELLIGENCE SUMMARY.
(Erase heading not required.)

Place	Date	Hour	Summary of Events and Information	Remarks and references to Appendices
LART	1/1/18		Moved off from LART at 12.45 a.m. and marched to WIZERNES where we arrived at	HAZEBROUCK
CANAL BANK	2/1/18		Detrained at ST JEAN at 11.0 a.m. Battalion dropped area at CANAL BANK	B.E.F. SHEET 2H.
"	3/1/18		The usual programme was carried out. Some slight shelling of the CANAL BANK by H.V. guns. The usual training programme was carried out	
	4/1/18		The usual programme of work was carried out. Officers reconnoitred the line	
	5/1/18		The usual programme was carried out.	
	6/1/18		Parade Service was held for the whole company.	
	7/1/18		The usual programme was carried out in the morning. Sports for the afternoon	
	C.1.18			
	8.1.18		2 of our platoons from the line. Coy moved off at 1 p.m. for Canal Bank to relieve 117 M.G. Coy in the WALLEMOLEN sector of the line. Coy. H.Q'rs moved to ALBERTA C11.c.8.6. Relief was carried out successfully	Sheet 28
ALBERTA	9.1.18		Some snow fell during the night. There was little artillery	

WAR DIARY or INTELLIGENCE SUMMARY

Army Form C. 2118.

Place	Date	Hour	Summary of Events and Information	Remarks and references to Appendices
ALBERTA C.11.c.36	9.1.18		activity. 3000 rounds were expended in harassing fire at night.	B+F SHEET 28
"	10.1.18		Hostile artillery quiet, 2 men were wounded by a shell at the gun position at BANFF HOUSE. 4000 rounds were fired on the usual targets at night.	
"	11.1.18		Hostile artillery was more active, especially from noon to 4 P.M. when a heavy barrage was put down on the Corps line at Bash Avem. 7000 rounds were fired at night.	
"	12.1.18		The day was quiet. 7000 rounds were fired in harassing fire.	
"	13.1.18		Officers of 116 company reconnoitred the line. That was some hostile artillery activity against batteries holding the Corps line. 8000 rounds were fired at night.	
"	14.1.18		Hostile artillery was quite. 12,000 rounds were fired to cover the infantry in a minor enterprise. 3000 rounds were fired in harassing fire on the usual targets.	
"	15.1.18		Hostile artillery more active, especially in the morning. Very heavy return fire at night & the chief shots were	

WAR DIARY
or
INTELLIGENCE SUMMARY

(Erase heading not required.)

Army Form C. 2118.

Instructions regarding War Diaries and Intelligence Summaries are contained in F. S. Regs., Part II. and the Staff Manual respectively. Title pages will be prepared in manuscript.

Place	Date	Hour	Summary of Events and Information	Remarks and references to Appendices
ALBERTA	15.1.18		Flooded out.	R + F Sheet 525
	16.1.18		The Company was relieved by the 116 M.G.Coy. The relief was carried out with considerable difficulty owing to the flooded state of the country but was completed at 10AM. 1 man was wounded. The Company proceeded to SIEGE CAMP by light railway.	
SIEGE CAMP	17.1.18		The Company spent the day resting & cleaning up	
B.20.d.8.7	18.1.18		The moved programme was carried out	
	19.1.18		The Company spent the day in refitting & gun equipment.	
	20.1.18		The Company paraded for Divisional Review & were inspected by the C.O.	
	21.1.18		The Company proceeded by march route to HOUTKERQUE starting at 7.30AM arriving at 2PM. The morning was good. Two men fell out.	
HOUTKERQUE	22.1.18		The day was spent in cleaning & fitting equipment.	
E.13.d.1.0.	23.1.18		The Company paraded at 9.0AM & carried out the usual programme	

Army Form C. 2118.

WAR DIARY
or
INTELLIGENCE SUMMARY.
(Erase heading not required.)

Place	Date	Hour	Summary of Events and Information	Remarks and references to Appendices
HOUTKERQUE	24.1.18		The company paraded for Battle during the morning. In the afternoon the match against C coy 1/1 to Camb'd Regt in the Brigade Football Competition was played off. won 5-3	Sheet C 28.
E13d 1.0	25.1.18		The company moved off at 7.0am and entrained at Proven at 10am. Detrained at MERICOURT L'ABBE at 9.30pm and marched to billets at BRAY SUR SOMME arriving at 1am 26.1.18.	AMIENS 1/100,000
BRAY	26.1.18		The company spent the day resting, cleaning up.	
	27.1.18		The usual programme was carried out. In the afternoon we played the B.W. in the semi-final of the football competition. Lost 2-1.	
	28.1.18		Preparation for the move. 2 officers reconnoitred the line.	
	29.1.18		Moved off at 11.30am and entrained at PLATEAU at 2.15pm. Detrained at PERONNE at 3.30pm and marched to camp at HAUT ALLAINES	
SORELLE GRAND	30.1.18		Moved off at 11.30am proceeded by road route to billets at SOREL LE GRAND.	SHEET 57B
	31.1.18		Preparation for line. Advance party went into the line.	

T.O.? W? Lt Col M?

CONFIDENTIAL

War Diary

of

118th Machine Gun Company.

from 1st February 1918 to 28th February 1918.

(Volume II)

Army Form C. 2118.

WAR DIARY
or
INTELLIGENCE SUMMARY.
(Erase heading not required.)

Place	Date	Hour	Summary of Events and Information	Remarks and references to Appendices
Sqdt. O.296 O.8.0 O.29	1st Feb.	2.30pm	The Coy. moved from Sect. 6. Canvel to the line "12 guns occupying front line" having to take over of Artillery accommodation to the sector generally & the remaining 6 guns with No. 6 Div reserve Battalions. Guns were in action with No 1,3,9,2 as attached to the Inniskillings No. 2 & 9 Chinquers & Guns No. 2 & No. 4 & No. 5 & No. 7 Butts. The Relief was completed nearly without incident & reliefs commenced by 6.15 pm.	Sheet 57 C 1/10 Coy. wore 1/10.000
	2 Feb		Day spent in settling into new positions. The line 9 zone blue primarily enemy observed & very able to do a fair bit of shell fire. Our own fire was hurrying in the three most Iron bound zone two men were able to keep up successive & continuous fire in all our three zones. Our fire was very fairly thus was before the attention during the 24 hours spent in observations.	General Kiroi & Weather Sand
2 Feb 26			Close succession by any of the 9 guns, where any direct hit was obtained. They were encountered & came under. On the Cox 1 gun attached to former monetary receivables & the dug outer fired which had informants concerned. We do up with Bull of surrounded in the Inn rocks were which seemed to excuse the avoidance of a fun guns the two attendance to sketch perfect neighborhood. The Cox came under shell fire between 11 am & 1 pm & 2 pm 8 our trenches	Weather adverse in progress

WAR DIARY or INTELLIGENCE SUMMARY

Army Form C. 2118.

Place	Date	Hour	Summary of Events and Information	Remarks and references to Appendices
Q.29.a.8.0.	3/2/18	cont	[continued from previous]	Gauche Wood 3/1/0 000
"	4/2/18		The day was quiet with only little artillery activity. Observers noticed nil unusual throughout the day but much hostile billet activity from Bn gun positions. Between 5 & 6 pm a number of contact aeroplanes were observed flying over the line. Hostile guns firing on Q.2.B., Q.8. & Q.P.28, Q.Q.2.a.&.c. were active. Our 18 pdrs & 4.5" How's replied. The enemy was firing up rockets but with no apparent answer. His artillery was slightly more active than usual. Nothing else to report.	
"	5/2/18	5.25AM	The Blackwatch tried to establish two small posts just forward of the old front line but were discovered and driven back by the enemy with M.G. fire. The posts were withdrawn. The operations carried out by 2nd Gordons to establish 5 small posts on our front have been carried out successfully. No casualties. Enemy guns a little more active than usual.	
"		5.0-7pm	000's were put down to the Right of I.Q.3.c.40.20. Neutralising charges were also brought down on a buzzing gun near R.28.c.75.15. Neither our Bn artillery activity during the night 4/5 inst.	
"	6/2/18		Not much artillery activity during the night 5/6 inst.	
			I.4.2. & 77mm were sent over in the vicinity of J. Posts L.S. with out claiming any damage.	cont-con 5/2/18

Army Form C. 2118.

WAR DIARY
or
INTELLIGENCE SUMMARY.
(Erase heading not required.)

Instructions regarding War Diaries and Intelligence Summaries are contained in F. S. Regs., Part II. and the Staff Manual respectively. Title pages will be prepared in manuscript.

118TH MACHINE GUN [stamp]
No. 15 G...

Place	Date	Hour	Summary of Events and Information	Remarks and references to Appendices
Q20.a.8.0	6/2/18		cont- This front observed a certain amount of alteration from M.G. fire early in the evening from the direction of Gonnelieu but this died down as soon as our M.G. opened fire with such effect. 1250 rounds being fired.	guide wire 1/12/17
"	7/2/18		An extremely quiet day with hardly a shot being fired. Harassing fire was continuous during the night 2500 rounds being fired on S.O.S. Targets at R26d 27.09 R26d 30.30 & R32 & 80.15	weather mild
"	8/2/18		Another relatively quiet day with the Machines chiefly in action. Harassing fire S.O.S. lines etc. 2 accounted for 2 to the N.E. current near Coy H.Q. Harassing was commenced with a rum ration at 2500 rounds being fired on harassing targets at R32d 20.17, R26d 75.10 - R26d 21.20	weather dull
"	9/2/18		The day was very quiet until 2.30pm when a number of 5.9"&4.2" were put on in the Rattle trenches G29a, G30c Also the shelling extended to the woollen 6a yards Onwards on Q86a. This was the most severe shelling there has ever been. After 2 & 1/2 hours ...	

D. D. & L., London, B.C.
(A.7889) Wt. W80/M1672 350,000 4/17 Sch. 82a. Forms/C/2118/14

Army Form C. 2118.

No. 160

WAR DIARY
or
INTELLIGENCE SUMMARY.
(Erase heading not required.)

Instructions regarding War Diaries and Intelligence Summaries are contained in F. S. Regs., Part II. and the Staff Manual respectively. Title pages will be prepared in manuscript.

Place	Date	Hour	Summary of Events and Information	Remarks and references to Appendices
Q29a80	11/2/18		cont— R28c.10.20 R22k.to.18 R28a.75.15 from M.G. Batty & batteries 2.000 rounds each to harass M.G.s & working parties. The 110th & 111th Coys of	
"			M.G. & machine gun Corps also	
"		06.10	Enemy artillery commenced active retaliation upon & near the village. This included Gas shells.	
"			Medium [...] [illegible] positions at Q.30c40c30. A much heavier shelling than the previous [...]	
"			7.00 Villg-on-10. The shelling continued until 4.22.6.30 at this time 2 or 3 heavy shells fell very heavily until 5.9.6.00 shells. There were no casualties. [...] [enemy]	
"			Questions from our [...] pouring at Q.38a with HE shells [...]	
"			some time. The neighbourhood of Fauquemer [...] were not shelled [...]	
"			[illegible] No Nos. 25.0.	
"		11.40	There was a demonstration shelling on the ground south of [...] at 11.25.a 3.0 throughout the day but [...] returning quiet.	
"			Relieved in the left place at dusk by 2 companies A.C.J. Cavalry M.G. during [...] [the] shelling	
"			[no] casualties. Weather dry.	
"	12/2/10		Quiet in quiet day. yesterday there was considerable shelling & [...] around [...]	
"			The morning of [...] Battery, but no damage or casualties. The [...]	
"			[...] taken [...] during the night	"

Army Form C. 2118.

No. 161

WAR DIARY
or
INTELLIGENCE SUMMARY
(Erase heading not required.)

Place	Date	Hour	Summary of Events and Information	Remarks and references to Appendices
Q29a5.0	13/2/18		The day as usual passed very quietly excepting for heavy artillery fire on both sides. Enemy aeroplane proceeded on their reconnaissance during the evening. Weather misty but clearing towards evening	Trench Map 1/10,000
"	14/2/18		Day quiet, a fair days work on the improvement of trenches has been done during the fine hours clearing mostly in the evening of a slight enemy aerial reconnaissance was seen. A fire at the Boche hangar has been brought down by the enemy enemy aeroplane broke down. Weather mostly bright and dry	
"	15/2/18	4pm	About 12 A.A. were put over in the near of Peurgaulin at Q.30a.40 but no occurrence was done	
		3pm-4.30pm	Three T.M. shelled the line at a great height	
		5.15pm	One S.A. crossed the line from Formelin at about 1500-2000 ft. One A.A. gun at R25a.30.60 engaged it immediately & fired about 65 rounds but no decisive result was obtained. Weather good.	
"	16/2/18	11am	4 T.D. com were chaffed beside the bunker used in 35.b.9.36.a offence at pounds Q35b.8.7.72.-Q35b.9.06-Q36a.0.7 at intervals of two minutes. Results were very good & the enemy balloons were suddenly drawing working parties at the point	

WAR DIARY or INTELLIGENCE SUMMARY

Army Form C. 2118.

Place	Date	Hour	Summary of Events and Information	Remarks and references to Appendices
			continued	Touch Wood Mr. vow
Q29A 8.0	16/2/18	1.57-a.m	Four shells were fired one close together H.Q. one falling about a couple of yards from the dugout. In both cases the dugouts were damaged slightly but there were no casualties.	
		7am-2am	Between 7am and 2am an E.A. came within range of Jem A.A. gun at R21a as or as immediately opened fire & the plane turned & made off. No ammunition fired. No enemy aircraft observed.	
		7.9 am	7.9 am from R20a3.5 but no results were observed.	Weather cold but visibility & sun good
17/2/18			An exceptionally quiet day, nothing particular occurred 2/Lt Butler proceeded leave	Weather intelligence
18/2/18			Very little activity within visibility a mist, all planes being out of range from J.A.	
		6 pm	Aero machine Gun information received from the D.M.G.O. word were about the Bradley R25a 3.5. 2500 rounds were fired on enemy troops moving on R83c & Northwood	
19/2/18		11.30am	Aerial Activity. A flight of 5 E.A. were observed to cross our lines. Weather continued fine from R25a 3.5 approached in a northerly direction at about 10000ft up. At 12 noon were chased by one of our planes. Our machine was 3 machines fought over Gommecourt. Enemy M.G.s were active at dusk at R25 a 3.5 approx.	Weather bright & clear

Army Form C. 2118.

WAR DIARY
or
INTELLIGENCE SUMMARY.
(Erase heading not required.)

Instructions regarding War Diaries and Intelligence Summaries are contained in F. S. Regs., Part II, and the Staff Manual respectively. Title pages will be prepared in manuscript.

Place	Date	Hour	Summary of Events and Information	Remarks and references to Appendices
Q29.a.8.0.	20th 1.16		The day was exceptionally quiet. There was a certain amount of casual activity on the part of the enemy but in intense form A.A. guns	Caurels Wood 1/40,000
	21 Feb 1918		Slight amount of activity on A.A. guns at R31 c or 05 fired 250 rounds at our S.A. at 10 a.m. caused it to alter its course. Otherwise the day was quiet	Weather good with a change
	22/2/18	2pm	5. 77mm fell at R25 a 3.7 m clear fire only. L.B.Battery but receiving no damage	Weather changeable wet
			Enemy M.G. was active in this area on this hour. The day was to quiet for enemy activity	same rain
	23/2/18			Weather cloudy with a high wind
			More shelling activity than on previous days, but the shells were mostly small 77m etc. a realised our fire generally. They obtained a direct hit on a dug-out in the Lembres Road.	
			in R31.b 5 were killed & wounded. Enemy M.G. were active at check at R25 a 30.50 answered.	
	24/2/18		A normal day, with little shelling on the front.	Weather fairly fair & warm
	25/2/18		A fair amount of shelling in the area during the day in a general way, a the usual M.G. fire, no casualties to the coy on enemy's done	Weather very warm
	26/2/18		Very little shelling during the 24 hours, enemy M.G. were less active than formerly	Weather continued good
			There was much activity on Patrol activity. Tn 6.30 am - 7.15 am am S.O.S. (our R.E.8 with our sign)	

WAR DIARY
or
INTELLIGENCE SUMMARY

Army Form C. 2118.

Place	Date	Hour	Summary of Events and Information	Remarks and references to Appendices
Q29 a 30	26/2/18		Comm an/s patrols between our lines & Ganges our outlying Posts billets etc	Cancelled Wires 1/1/18, 1/2
			front line. We engaged & drove off night anemature	
	27/2/18		Quiet generally, at intermittent intervals throughout the day the enemy put over 10cm	Weather Good
			shells into area about Q36b 20.20	
		1.30pm	6 x 2 HE burst in Q30 a & at continued there were bursts 8.6 77m about R19c 50 vo	
		1.55pm	2 EA approached from a NE direction & turned over R25a b went N 2 aeroplanes	
			fired Klaxon & [?]	
		1.30pm	An LA with Hun marks a gens appeared from the enemy lines a fired into our front line	Weather Fair
			It was chased from our at R25 c 55 60 & R25c 20 35 a	
			A successful barrage was carried out by the 1/6 Cheshires assisted by the artillery &	
			MG. at 5.15am. We on fired 27,930 rounds during the operations which lasted 15 min. &	
			enemy retaliation was not great & there was no casualties	Weather very Hot & sunny
	28/2/18			
				C.O. Boadich Lt.
				M.O.
				1/8 Bn. M.G.C.
	1/3/18			

WO95/2591-5

118 Bde T.M. Batty -

Jul - Aug 1916

39 Div - 118 Inf Bde

39TH DIVISION
118TH INFY BDE

TRENCH MORTAR BTY
JLY - AUG 1916.

To/ 30th June 1916
116th Infantry Brigade

Operations.

No. 2. 3.7" Light Trench Mortar opened fire at 3.20 a.m. with smoke shells. At 3.27 am No 2 gun was put out of action by the bolt connecting the base plate to the Barrel breaking in a half ho. Gun carried on until 5 a.m when the Rifle mechanism blew out putting the gun out of action.

30/6/16.

Saville 2nd Lieut
118th T.M.B

Ammunition left handed over to O/c Company holding the line

SECRET.

Headquarters,

    39th Division.

    Reference your message A.522 dated August 18th, herewith War Diary of T.M. Battery for July.

                                     Brigadier-General,
19/8/16.   Commanding 118th Infantry Brigade.

Secret and Confidential

HEADQUARTERS A.A. & Q.M.G.
Date ....
No. 39/1197/A
39th DIVISION

D.A.G.
3rd Echelon Base,

Forwarded in continuation of this Office letter No. 39/1197/A dated 4.8.16. Duplicate copy is being retained for reference.

Will you kindly acknowledge.

19 8/16

E.A. Childe-Thomas. Major
for A.A.Q. 39' Division

No. 1
Army Form C. 2118.
July Vol. I

WAR DIARY
INTELLIGENCE SUMMARY
(Erase heading not required.)

89 / 118th Trench Mortar Battery

Place	Date	Hour	Summary of Events and Information	Remarks and references to Appendices
Villa Chapelle	1/7/16		Moved from billets at Vielle Chapelle to Richebourg. Took over from 184th T.M.B. in the Ferme du Bois Sector at 6 P.M. Enemy active during the hanaques 10.45 P.M.	
	2/7/16		Quiet day & night. We fired a few rounds during the afternoon.	
	3/7/16		Quiet day & night.	
	4/7/16		Quiet day & night. New targets registered during the day.	
	5/7/16		Intermittent firing carried out on enemy front line during the evening. Slight retaliation.	
	6/7/16		Relieved by 184th T.M.B. Moved from Richebourg to Vielle Chapelle.	
	7/7/16		Moved from Vielle Chapelle to Gorre. Took over from 98th T.M.B. in Givenchy Sector & 116th in Festubert Sector.	
	8/7/16		Two guns opened hyper at 6 P.M. on right centre Coy. in Givenchy Sector. No firing took place owing to relief of Battalion in the line.	
	9/7/16		Guns registered. Two direct hits obtained on Snipers post.	
	10/7/16		Fired on another Snipers post with good results.	
	11/7/16		Fired twenty five rounds on enemy Gates & Trenches. Enemy was quick in retaliation with Rifle grens & "Rum Jars"; large proportion of his shells were "duds".	

Army Form C. 2118.

WAR DIARY
INTELLIGENCE SUMMARY.
(Erase heading not required.)

No. 14.

Instructions regarding War Diaries and Intelligence Summaries are contained in F.S. Regs., Part II. and the Staff Manual respectively. Title pages will be prepared in manuscript.

Place	Date	Hour	Summary of Events and Information	Remarks and references to Appendices
	11/9/16		Enemy were active with Rifle grenades. We retaliated with 108 rounds during the day which succeeded in silencing them.	
	12/9/16		Enemy were again active during the day with Rifle Grenades, but ceased after we fired twenty five rounds.	
	13/9/16		Quiet day.	
	14/9/16		Enemy Snipers were active during the day. We fired on snipers' posts causing slight retaliation, to which we replied with further Stokes shells until the enemy was silenced.	
	15/9/16		Our Artillery was active during the afternoon.	
	16/9/16		Enemy Artillery was active during the day as an O.P. Trench Raids carried out on Enemy trench line during the night. Stokes Coy fired 100 rounds. Fired a 3.7" trench mortar.	
	17/9/16		Bombs in Festubert Sector.	
	18/9/16		Our Artillery again Bombarded enemy front line over for four & half hours.	
	20/9/16		Quiet day.	

Army Form C. 2118.

WAR DIARY
or
INTELLIGENCE SUMMARY.
(Erase heading not required.)

No. 3

Instructions regarding War Diaries and Intelligence Summaries are contained in F.S. Regs., Part II. and the Staff Manual respectively. Title pages will be prepared in manuscript.

Place	Date	Hour	Summary of Events and Information	Remarks and references to Appendices
	26/6/16		Quiet day. Fired one hundred fifty rounds in Guinchy Sector in support of raid on the Northern Craters. Smoke Barrage in student sector cancelled, owing to unfavorable wind.	
	27/6/16			
	28/6/16		Quiet day. Few rounds fired on Enemy trenches.	
	29/6/16		Fired seventy rounds on Enemy front + Support lines. Retaliation was weak.	
	30/6/16			
	1/7/16		Relieved by 119th T.M.B. Marched out 8:30. Billets in Bethune.	
	2/7/16		Bethune. " "	
	3/7/16		" "	
	4/7/16		" "	
	5/7/16		" "	

Bentley 2nd Lieut
118th T.M.B 3/7/16

Army Form C. 2118.

WAR DIARY
INTELLIGENCE SUMMARY
(Erase heading not required.)

115: Trench Mortar Battery

Vol 2

Instructions regarding War Diaries and Intelligence Summaries are contained in F. S. Regs., Part II. and the Staff Manual respectively. Title pages will be prepared in manuscript.

Place	Date	Hour	Summary of Events and Information	Remarks and references to Appendices
	August 1916			
FESTUBERT	1/8/16		Marched from BETHUNE to Headquarters at le TOURET & billeted with 116th LTMB and in FESTUBERT sector. Quiet day	
	2/8/16		Quiet day.	
	3/8/16		Enemy shelled our Communication trenches during the afternoon. Fired on enemy front line. Slight retaliation	
	4/8/16		Quiet day	
	5/8/16		Enemy shelled Battery in rear of our lines.	
	6/8/16		Enemy again shelled Battery in rear from lines	
	7/8/16		Went over the line with O/C 93rd T.M.B.	
	8/8/16		Quiet day	
	9/8/16			
	10/8/16		Relieved by 93rd LTMB Marched into Billets in BETHUNE	
	11/8/16		Marched from BETHUNE to COUCHY A LA TOUR	
	12/8/16		Marched from COUCHY A LA TOUR to ROCOURT	
	13/8/16		Marched from ROCOURT to BETHONSART and took over Billets	
	14/8/16		Training	
	15/8/16		"	

Army Form C. 2118.

WAR DIARY
or
INTELLIGENCE SUMMARY.
(Erase heading not required.)

119¼ T.M.B.

Instructions regarding War Diaries and Intelligence Summaries are contained in F. S. Regs., Part II. and the Staff Manual respectively. Title pages will be prepared in manuscript.

Place	Date	Hour	Summary of Events and Information	Remarks and references to Appendices
BETHONSART	16/8/16		Training	
"	17/8/16		"	
"	18/8/16		"	
"	19/8/16		Lecture on bayonet fighting	
"	20/8/16		Flammenwerfer demonstration	
"	21/8/16		Training	
"	22/8/16		"	
"	23/8/16		Marched from BETHONSART to CANETTEMONT	
CANETTEMONT	24/8/16		Marched from CANETTEMONT to HALLOY	
HALLOY	25/8/16		Marched from HALLOY to BUS-LES-ARTOIS	
BUS-LES-ARTOIS	26/8/16		Marched from BUS-LES-ARTOIS to billets in Mailly-Maillet Wood & took over	
MAILLY-MAILLET	27/8/16		line from 138 T.M.B. in Sector North of THIEPVAL	
"	28/8/16		Considerable artillery activity on enemy lines	
"	29/8/16		Do	
"	30/8/16		"	
"	31/8/16		"	

Davies
119¼ T.M.B.
31st August 1916

T.J134. Wt. W708—776. 500000. 4/15. Sir J. C. & S.

www.ingramcontent.com/pod-product-compliance
Lightning Source LLC
Chambersburg PA
CBHW080854230426
43662CB00013B/2099